The Reinvention Equation

A Boomer's Guide to a Reinvented Life

Howard J. Parsons

BALBOA.
PRESS
A DIVISION OF HAY HOUSE

Balboa Press books may be ordered through booksellers or by contacting:

Balboa Press
A Division of Hay House
1663 Liberty Drive
Bloomington, IN 47403
www.balboapress.com
1 (877) 407-4847

Because of the dynamic nature of the Internet, any web addresses or
links contained in this book may have changed since publication and
may no longer be valid. The views expressed in this work are solely those
of the author and do not necessarily reflect the views of the publisher,
and the publisher hereby disclaims any responsibility for them.

The author of this book does not dispense medical advice or prescribe the use
of any technique as a form of treatment for physical, emotional, or medical
problems without the advice of a physician, either directly or indirectly. The
intent of the author is only to offer information of a general nature to help
you in your quest for emotional and spiritual well-being. In the event you use
any of the information in this book for yourself, which is your constitutional
right, the author and the publisher assume no responsibility for your actions.

Any people depicted in stock imagery provided by Thinkstock are models,
and such images are being used for illustrative purposes only.
Certain stock imagery © Thinkstock.

Print information available on the last page.

ISBN: 978-1-5043-7193-3 (sc)
ISBN: 978-1-5043-7195-7 (hc)
ISBN: 978-1-5043-7194-0 (e)

Library of Congress Control Number: 2016921020

Balboa Press rev. date: 01/05/2017

Contents

Acknowledgments

Gratitude is the word that comes to mind over and over again when I think of the people who have had an influence on my life and who have had a hand in making this book a reality.

The events of our lives shape and guide us on our journeys, so I know the essence of this book, which is based on my experiences, has been unfolding within me for many years. This book could not be a reality without all the jobs I have had, the clients I have worked with, and the traumas I have gone through and survived. It is with gratitude that I look back on my history and the richness these experiences have contributed to my life.

Thanks to Blaine Skleryk of Laser Health for realigning my body and introducing me to the study of somatics, which became a central part of my research for this book.

Martha Peterson, a guru of somatics and author of *Move without Pain*, has been very kind and generous with her time in helping me to deepen my study of somatics and the connection between our brains and our bodies. Thank you, Martha, for the contribution you have made to this work.

To my daughter, Nikki, thank you for being my teacher and inspiring me to be better in all respects.

Finally, my heart is alive with love and gratitude for my wife, Kerry. For over thirty years she has supported me, inspired me, and honored who I am as no other. Thank you, my love.

With the deepest gratitude for what life offers each of us, I invite you to embrace your own life journey.

Introduction

How do we face reinvention of our lives? How do we let go of all we were taught and break through to create new life patterns? How do we create lives that are way more satisfying than the ones we have lived up to now?

I have spent the last thirty years trying to find answers to these questions through my career as a corporate executive and the consulting work I have done with men and women in the middle of life transitions. I've noticed that such transitions are particularly difficult for baby boomers. This realization led to me writing this book, which is targeted specifically to baby boomers, those of us born between 1946 and 1964.

We baby boomers were taught to get an education, work hard for one company for our entire careers, get married, have kids, and make sure we had pension plans. If we did all this, then at age fifty-five all would be fine. We grew up in a world economically exploding in the postwar boom. People all over the world were becoming more prosperous than ever before. Advanced technology came into our homes in the form of television. Our world seemed like a place where we could have anything we wanted. All we had to do was apply ourselves to the task at hand and reap the rewards of our effort.

Over the years in which I've worked with baby boomers, I have experienced and witnessed the pain of living in a world that is not the one you expected. Careers have been shattered as companies reorganized to adjust to economic circumstances; divorce has become mainstream as disenchanted partners try to find new answers for their lives; and with stress levels having increased to the breaking point, health has become a major focus. Drugs and alcohol have become common tools with which to handle stress.

As one of my friends once told me, "We were sold a bill of goods by our parents!" Things were supposed to be straightforward, with the results of our lives matching the effort we put in to be good parents and employees. However, we must acknowledge and face the facts of the new world in which we now live. Old strategies no longer work. We cannot go looking for opportunities or relationships the way we once did ... from the outside in. This book is about bringing hope to baby boomers and anyone who wants to learn a new way to live. There is a way through to a new life more satisfying and fulfilling than you have lived up until now.

This book is about learning to reinvent your life from the inside out. This new way of living is opposite to the way we were trained and how our expectations were formed. We haven't had the language or scientific information until now to grasp how to reinvent from the inside out, but we can find hope in that there is a way to do so. In this book, I lay out a way to reinvent your life from the inside out using current technology and science. This method works, and you can learn it.

I decided to write this book based on my own experiences of divorce, job loss, alcoholism, and cancer and the pain those experiences caused me. It has taken me time to look inside myself to see what new way might be possible. In doing so, I have been honored to work with men and women seeking to create their lives from the inside out.

My dad was a hardworking doctor, and my mother was a visionary and energetic community builder. She, in particular, taught me I could be whatever I wanted to be. Success came early in my life with school and community recognition for my positive attitude and increasing sales on my paper route. These seem like simple stories, yet to a baby boomer of ten years old they were life affirming.

When I graduated from university, I went to work for the government, with my new bride by my side. She was finishing her master's degree, and together we made plans to take on the world. She'd learned about life from her dad, a Second World War vet and a farmer. He'd taught her loyalty and dogged determination and to never give up no matter what circumstances were thrown at her. We thought we had the makings of a winning team. Our marriage lasted fourteen years. In the midst of our breakup, I came face-to-face with my old strategies of denial, blame, and emotional disconnection. However, even this traumatic event was not enough for me to see I needed to do my life differently.

We baby boomers have a particular definition of ourselves rooted in praise, hard work, and pursuit of opportunity. But the world changed while we were caught up in making the best lives we could. Local economies transformed into a global economy seemingly overnight. Companies once thought to be stable were gobbled up by bigger players in their markets, resulting in layoffs never thought possible in the past. The global price of commodities began to influence local companies, and as a result employment levels went up and down with the changing prices of those commodities. Japan went from producing junk products to producing some of the highest-quality products on the planet. Jobs were shifted overseas in a quiet but steady wave, and jobs that had existed for many years in the United States disappeared. Career planning for us boomers became a traumatic experience because we were knocked out of our comfort zone of being able to move from one similar job to another as we worked our way up the corporate ladder. The world had changed beyond what we had been taught to expect. It went from a world we knew and were comfortable in to one in which we were lost as to how to navigate in the new global economy.

The world has grown more complex and faster moving, rocking baby boomers to the core. Our hearts have been cracked open with the realization that we live in a new world not all of us understand. The need to reinvent lives we thought were going to be solid and prosperous is not optional anymore. Learning how to reinvent successfully from the inside out and not the outside in is now a necessity. As I studied this phenomenon through personal experience and with my clients, I developed tools and skills to make reinvention a positive experience.

It has taken me a long time and a number of years to face the reality of our world's new circumstances, but that, I think, is the baby boomer mentality. We have tried to keep the status quo because it is what we know.

In this book I will teach you the difference between your adapted self and your essential self and the part each of these aspects play in your reinvention.

Through my experiences of thirty-four years of drinking, starting at the age of fourteen; divorce; and cancer, my heart has been cracked open several times. I have experienced and undertaken the process of reinvention to reveal to me the light and wisdom that each one of us is, if we choose to see it and use it.

This book covers the study of neuroscience and the positive ways this knowledge can be used to change the patterns in our brains and therefore the patterns of our lives. We all have self-talk and ways of acting that have been ingrained in us for many years. For example, I learned early on how to shut down my emotions. To this day, given circumstances involving stress or conflict, I can shut down my feeling nature and go into denial about what is really happening.

Our brains are amazing and complex computers made up of billions of electrical connections in a weblike formation. In the old days scientists thought that the brain was fixed and hardwired and that it depreciated in capability as we got older. We now know this theory is incorrect. The brain is actually very pliable. You have the ability to rewire your brain, and hopefully this knowledge will give you confidence to reinvent your life in a creative, sustainable way you might not have thought about before.

In this book you will see the reinvention equation has two parts. The first part lays the foundation for understanding how adapted we became as children and covers some of the science around how to change your brain and the life-long patterns you have been using.

Gratitude is one of the tools you will learn to use. I am grateful for all the bumps in the road I have experienced because without them I never would have found a way to reinvent my life. Self-compassion is something many of us do not know much about but should. To deeply love others, you must first develop a deep love of yourself.

The second part is where we get down to work and the rubber meets the road, so to speak. I will take you through the specific skills you need to master to activate and mobilize the reinvention equation for yourself. I'll also present the obstacles you will meet and how to work around them with loving kindness. My passion is to help you live the best possible life you can, no matter what your background or experience. The brain is accessible to change to anyone who learns how to work with it and practices with the tools to make it happen. You have a lot of experience and skills you may not have put into action yet to bring to the reinvention party. There is a lot of living to do from here on out. Let's go!

To change your behaviors and therefore your life's results, you need three things:

1. Information
2. Skill proficiency at understanding and changing neural patterns
3. Regular practice

This book lays out the steps and skills you need to reinvent your life in a way that will enhance your experiences for all the years you have left. I know these scientific, intellectual, and emotional methods work because I have used them myself to create a life in which I live with gratitude. You have the power to reinvent your life. Take the first step, and the path will appear. I guarantee it.

Chapter 1

The Backstory

Days are expensive. When you spend a day you have one less day to spend. So make sure you spend each one wisely.

—Jim Rohn

When you hold a new baby, you see a miracle. There is no doubt babies are perfect little beings arriving in our arms as bundles of joy; possibility; and pure, unadulterated love. How could we see them as anything less than perfect?

We know in our hearts they are connected to their essential beings. We see there are no walls or obstacles between a baby and its essence. Some might say we see the soul of the baby because a baby's form is so pure. We all have a sense of purity and clarity that we remember about ourselves—the essential self that we separated from soon after our births. A new baby we hold in our arms is us so many years ago.

The Adaptation Process

Babies only maintain their connection to their essential selves for a short time. When they arrive, they must learn to live in a new environment that is harsh compared to where they have spent the previous nine months. This is the beginning of the adaptation process. Every one of us comes into this world with the ability to adapt. Babies are in survival mode when they are first born. The delivery team and mom and dad hold their breath as the new baby struggles to take its first breath of life outside the womb.

A baby's first breath is probably the most difficult breath the baby will ever take in its life. While in the womb, babies' lungs are filled with fluid, and when a baby takes its first breath, it has to replace this fluid with air. The complex process of exchanging fluid for air is an extremely vital and necessary physical adaptation the baby must make in its first minutes of life outside the womb. This faculty of adaptation is a powerful and useful one for us. As we age, we all undertake adaptation not only on a physical level but also on emotional and intellectual levels.

We learn at a very early age how to adapt our ways of acting, feeling, and thinking as we encounter the circumstances of our lives. For example, babies learn quickly to cry in order to get attention or to be fed. Babies also learn what garners a positive reaction and what brings a negative response from their parents. For the most part, our adapted behaviors become unconscious because we get so used to reacting in a particular way to the circumstances of our lives. Then these adaptations become habitual patterns that repeat over and over during our lifetimes unless we become aware of them and how they may or may not be serving us.

Adapted Journey—A Journey of Survival

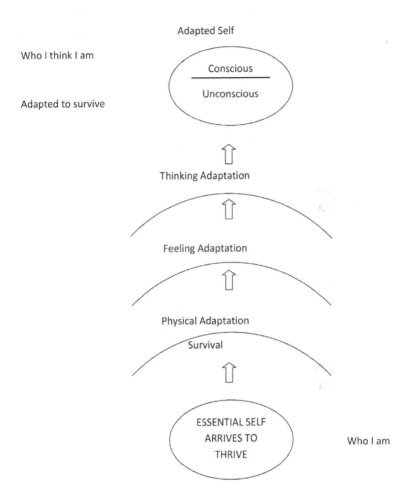

One of the adaptive strategies I took with me into adulthood was a fear of conflict. I would not confront friends, coworkers, or bosses if they were not respecting me or if they were creating situations in which I felt inadequate. Whenever possible, I would work alone rather than be on a team because the buildup of internal stress from avoidance of conflict was difficult to handle. As a result, in my working career, even though I managed to work my way close to the top, I became drained, depressed, and ill by the time I was fifty years of age. This is a pattern I see in many baby boomers. We were brought up in an expanding economy, and we had self-expectations of loyalty, longevity of employment, and financial success. Many of us worked hard at building our families and careers without noticing how we were using the habits we had learned as children. Here we are now in our fifties and sixties still trying to use old strategies. We have the mind-set "The tougher life gets, the harder I will work because that is what I know." This brings us to the first stage of the reinvention equation: Stop! Take time to inventory your life with two questions:

1. Who am I?
2. Where am I?

Sensory Emotional Amnesia

Neuroscience studies have revealed how brain neurons function and how they interact within an intricate weave of billions of connections. In terms of the science of the brain, we are barely breaking the surface of the most complex and powerful part of the human body. However, much has been learned in the past decade that can help you on the journey of reinvention. One of these discoveries is the pliable nature of the neural structure of the brain.

Our adaptive habitual patterns learned through years of training in our families and communities have us act, feel, and think in ways that are familiar to us. In my case, as I was growing up, I decided it was not okay to express sadness, so that emotion went underground. That way of dealing with feelings lasted many years. So when my divorce happened, I had no conscious way of finding the feeling of sadness. I had forgotten that it is normal to express a wide range of feelings. The feedback loop between my brain and feelings was stuck in a particular neural pattern. I will discuss this in more detail later, but for now it is enough to know that the default for me was always to shut down my feelings of sadness when events occurred in which that emotion would be normal. This is what I call *sensory emotional amnesia*, a condition in which the neural patterns of the brain are such that certain feelings are not accessible until measures are taken to change the neural patterns. You can think of it like driving in a circle. You drive around and around not realizing there is any other way.

In order to make a change in our neural patterns and therefore a change in our lives, we need to recognize what is taking place and consciously choose to have a different experience. For example, in my family, anger was never shown or talked about. If I was angry, I learned to keep it to myself. This way of handling emotions is confusing to a child who initially believes that it's okay to express the way he or she feels. The idea of keeping certain feelings hidden is something children will not only learn but also use to evaluate what is okay to express and what must be kept within one's own heart in all situations, whether at home, play, or work. Keeping feelings hidden leads to stress within the body, and when young, we do not have the skills to release this stress.

At the company I worked for, we used to say, "Leave your personal life at home." We interpreted that to mean *Don't talk about your personal pain or family issues at the office.* Feelings were not welcomed when there was work to do. So the adaptation of locking away feelings and emotions continued. We told the stories of what happened at work and how we felt about various situations at outside parties or to friends with whom we felt safe. In some way we were trying to relieve the stress created by bottling up all the emotions that we felt. Those emotions were real. Our adaptation to what was required at work took a lot of energy to maintain, but we learned to do it at a huge cost to our emotional and physical health.

As children get older, they learn to understand the unstated rules of their families and surroundings. Learning how to play the game to get what they want is an important lesson for children, and it starts in the family environment. For example, if they eat all their supper, they get positive messages. If they don't eat certain foods, they get negative messages. Children think about how their families work before taking action so they can get what they so desperately want. Children will consciously throw screaming tirades, knowing their parents will give in to their demands.

Being a Team Player

As adults we know screaming won't work with our bosses, but we use strategies to make us feel a part of the team and to be seen as a team players. When we were one to three years old, we learned how to look like a team player at home. Now we are over fifty and employ strategies to accomplish the same result. The difficulty is that looking like a team player is not the same as feeling like a team player. So many of my generation go to work with their outside images not matching how they feel on the inside. It is a formula for illness inside and out, and this is why change is called for in the new world in which we find ourselves. Psychologists say children learn all their adapted strategies by the age of seven or earlier. The adaptations become locked in at an unconscious level and are then activated as needed in order to live in the family and later to get along in the world as an adult. Combined, sensory emotional amnesia and adaptation make us repeat life patterns over and over again. If you want to live your life fully aware and free to express a range of feelings, then you must develop an understanding of sensory emotional amnesia and adaptation.

A friend of mine has been separated from his wife for nine years. My friend's father was an alcoholic and would rage and abuse his wife when he was drunk. As a result, my friend learned as a child always to be nice to people and never to get into fights. My friend, at the age of six, started to take care of and protect his mom. As crazy as it might sound, this is not really an unreasonable decision for him to have made. He was attempting to take care of himself, and the way he saw to do that was to take care of his mom. I can only imagine the pain in this child's heart. He had no way of resolving the situation and shut down his feeling nature in order to handle what was going on in the family. That was how he became the nice guy. He made a decision when he was six years old to never hurt anyone in his life.

His learned adapted behavior to always be polite and avoid conflict created issues in his adult life. For years after he and his wife separated, he continued to support her financially. He had no capacity to speak for himself as to what he wanted and needed from the separation because he automatically operated as the nice guy. The pain of his past was buried deep inside, inaccessible to him. Therefore for a long time he did not start divorce proceedings. He increasingly felt chained to his past and unable to move on to a new relationship.

After some coaching he decided that he wanted to get the divorce finalized. This was a major decision because it would bring up conflict with his ex and bring him face-to-face with his old family patterns. After garnering the courage, he told her what he wanted, and she went into a rage. You can imagine his reaction as he was emotionally transported back to the times when his father raged.

However, with coaching, he stayed firm in his decision. Using techniques I will teach you in this book, he forged ahead with the divorce. For the first time since he and his wife were separated, he hired a lawyer to draw up the documents and have them served to her. This was a challenging time because it was a new path for him. He was going against everything he had learned about being nice. But with support from his coach and the use of specific techniques and practices to change lifelong patterns, he started to like himself more and began to free himself from the rubble of the past.

Our brains are fluid webs of electrical connections responding to events in any given moment. When we operate unconsciously from past experience, we get the same old results. Once we start making conscious choices, we are guaranteed to have new outcomes. Then the key is to strengthen the new, healthy patterns through practice.

My friend is now on his way to completing the divorce he has so long wanted. He is dating again and is consciously practicing being aware and mindful in his life. His pattern of life had nothing to do with being a nice guy and everything to do with adapted programming as a child.

We have all created adapted selves that we identify as who we are. I adapted to the way my family worked by keeping to myself, not revealing what I saw, and acting as though everything was fine when in reality it wasn't. Our adapted ways of living are only the ways we behave, not who we really are, our essential selves.

Somatics

Somatics is a methodology by which we can embody transformation, individually and collectively. Embodied transformation is foundational change that shows in our actions and our ways of being, relating, and perceiving. It is transformation that sustains over time.

Thomas Hanna, founder of the Association for Hanna Somatic Education, describes three primary reactions to events that have a direct impact on the body: green light, red light, and trauma.

The green-light response is one that tenses your body and prepares it for action. Your back muscles get tight, and you stand upright. At the emotional level you may feel excited and have a smile on your face. You react like a kid to what you perceive will be a positive experience.

In the red-light reaction, your body collapses inward for protection. You may be feeling fear, anxiety, or stress. Drawing from your memory bank, your brain creates an impulse to act in the same way that you did as a child. You may feel nausea, a tight stomach, or tears rising to the surface.

In the trauma reaction, your breath is taken away, your body becomes very tense, and you stop in your tracks. All your muscles tighten. Then you release and feel the stress of the moment. You start to think about what to do next. Your brain provides input based on what is in your memory bank, so the reaction is one of a child, based on what you learned to do in the face of trauma as a child. When I was fourteen, the death of my mother was a huge trauma. To cope, I shut down all my emotions because that was the behavior I had learned in the family. My body literally collapsed into itself as I sought isolation rather than connection to work through my loss.

The point is, as Hanna explains, nothing happens in our physical, emotional, or thinking bodies without communication from our brains. There is always a feedback loop working to coordinate and communicate what is happening and what needs to happen. When the feedback loop gets stuck in a pattern, the brain sends and receives the same signals over and over. At the physical level this shows up as pain in our muscles. If you sit at a desk all day, the neural pattern in your brain signals the appropriate muscles to contract in a certain way. If the pattern is continued long enough, the muscles will get sore because the signals back and forth from the brain to the muscles are in a continuous loop. The way you are sitting and the muscle pattern become so familiar that the pattern becomes unconscious. Hanna calls this sensory motor amnesia.

In this book, I have coined the terms *sensory emotional amnesia* and *sensory intellectual amnesia* because the adapted patterns we learn as children are played over and over again during our lives. At the emotional level, this shows up as always displaying the same emotions in a particular situation. An example of this is how I emotionally shut down, a pattern I had learned to deal with difficult situations, after my mother's death. The extremely close relationship she and I had was gone in an instant, leaving me with a vacuum in my life. I no longer had a context for my life. At the thinking level, adapted patterns show up as thinking inside the box or having a one-track mind without the awareness to expand one's thinking or look at alternatives. In each case, emotional and intellectual, it is not a question of the functions not being available; rather, the alternatives have been forgotten, or amnesia has set in, due to long-ago learning.

We are taught as children how to think and what to think and how to judge the people and the world around us. We also observe nonverbal messages in the interactions of our parents, siblings, and those around us. We do so in order to learn how things work in our world. We do the same thing when starting a new job, learning the written and unwritten rules as to how things work in this specific company. We learn how to adapt our behavior to fit into the culture of the organization. This seems simple and actually helpful, at least on the surface. However, because most of us have put aside our essential selves to fit into our families, we employ the same strategies at work. In the early years it is helpful to have learned a way to think about the world and how to handle it.

We have all been taught a way to think. This is not good nor bad; it is just the way we humans are brought up in order to function. However, over time sensory intellectual amnesia sets in, and we forget that we can look at situations from many different angles and can use a variety of methods to handle those situations. We become set in our ways of behavior. For example, the first thing I learned about any project was that work came before play. That meant I would work until my tasks for the day were completed, and then I could release myself to go and do something else.

When I took on the project of painting the exterior of my house, I dug into what I knew about painting. This was not a deep well of knowledge, yet having some confidence that what I'd learned over the years would serve me well, I got started. The painting project took about two weeks. Every day I planned out what I would do, how long I would work, and what supplies I would need. Having grown up with an attitude of wanting to do everything alone, I didn't ask for help or consult people I knew who were expert painters. Why would I? Can you spot the three adaptive patterns I was using in this project? The first one was believing that the work must be done before I could play. The second one was having a one-track mind. I got focused and stayed focused until the project was done. Unfortunately other tasks and people in my life got short shrift at times like this. The third adaptive strategy was doing it alone. I didn't want to ask for help because I had a notion that I would be criticized. These patterns were deeply rooted, old, and not serving me well any longer. However, sensory intellectual amnesia had set in to the extent that I did not consider other options as possibilities.

The Masks We Wear

Our adapted selves are who we think we are. Our essential selves or true selves become deeply hidden because we use our adapted behaviors and not our essential selves to make our way in the world. Trauma of some kind often functions as a wake-up call, providing the opening for us to examine and activate the essential part of us that has been put aside for a long, long time.

Our true selves are masked by our adaptations whether we know it or not. Our adaptations are at work all the time to keep us in sync with what we perceive the world needs from us. Our families, employers, children, and others all need us to behave in a certain way. Our egos are developed along the way, and the voices of our elders eventually become our own voices. These inner voices provide ongoing advice as to what to do when, where, and how along with criticism when we judge ourselves as doing it wrong.

Like a snake devouring a big meal, our generation has impacted every aspect of life. The huge bulge in population put pressure on the system for more schools and more services in both the public and private sectors, such as retail outlets. As the economy grew nationally and globally, there was an unprecedented opportunity for baby boomers to work around the world rather than just locally, but there were also unexpected challenges, like the outsourcing of jobs to other countries. Now that we are moving into middle age and becoming senior citizens, health care has become a major issue, as evidenced by the amount of money the government has had to allocate to take care of an aging population. The world has changed in ways we did not anticipate. The move from a local economy to a global economy means whatever happens in other countries has a direct impact on us locally. For example, the price of oil in Saudi Arabia affects the price here in America, which in turn has a direct bearing on jobs. The price of oil in world markets has declined significantly over the past two years. Oil-centered cities have seen a corresponding dramatic rise in unemployment as jobs have been cut and projects canceled. Many of the jobs lost were held by long-term baby boomer employees expecting to be employed until retirement. Now in midlife they are forced to find ways to live and work within circumstances that are not familiar to them. As an externally focused generation we thought life in our later years would be abundant, easy, and fun because we had put in the hard work and time to earn our leisure years. Now we must look to the resources we have within us to see what is possible in this new world.

You might feel as if the world has changed right before your eyes, like the changing world economy; however, you may or may not think it is a big deal—depending on how the changes affect you personally. At fourteen years old I turned away from the loss of a person I loved, my mother, and carried on as though nothing had changed. That was what I thought I was supposed to do, of course, based on my learning that emotions should not be shown. From this learning I'd come to the conclusion that emotions must not be important. Yet, at some level inside of me, I knew everything had changed. We know when our insides don't match our outsides. Our intuitions are strong and always accurate. However, many times we ignore our intuitions, which are the voices of our essential selves, and rely on our adapted selves, which also have voices. Our adapted selves' voices are usually loud and clear, and we are used to listening to them because they direct us every day.

Reinvention

When trauma occurs, we have the opportunity for reinvention. We have a choice: we can engage fully in the awareness of the trauma and choose to change the direction of our lives, or we can push away the feelings and carry on as though we have no changes to make.

I remember the day I was fired from my executive position. I had started as the local human resources manager and over ten years moved up to be the vice president overlooking the human resources function of five plants. My life was my job. A British conglomerate had purchased the company, so I often traveled internationally on special projects and teams. I had no idea who I was if a car and driver were not available to pick me up at the airport and take me to a first-class hotel. The adaptation process was fully engaged as I attempted to fit in and be one of the executive members everyone looked up to. The morning the president called me into his office, my stomach was churning, I knew something was up. These types of meetings are not usually long, and soon another senior manager was escorting me from the building. I had done this process with hundreds of employees over the years. One moment you feel like you are a part of something, and then you are walked out of the building because you a security risk. Coldness seeped through my bones as I went into shutdown, my adapted way of handling any emotional event.

This was the third time I lost context for my life. The first was when my mother died, and the second was when I went through a divorce. I drove away filled with the fear of not knowing the next step. Little did I know this was a perfect opportunity to reinvent myself in a way I had never thought of before.

If not addressed, our suffering is left inside and carried along as part of us, unseen and unacknowledged. For a long time I did not acknowledge my suffering in my executive career. I did not realize that for all those years I was using my adapted self to fit in, be liked, and be seen as a company man. It was a few years before I acknowledged the abusive culture I had tried to fit into every day. By being fired I was set free to explore my authentic potential, and for that reason I am grateful I was fired, because I never would have made the decision to leave on my own. This book is about reinvention and is inspired by my experiences and those of the clients

I have worked with and been inspired by over the years. Every one of us is unique and magnificent and has our place in society. However, the pleasures, the toys, the money, and the ways we are taught to relate with others play a huge role in how we cover up and ignore the truth of who we are.

Unless you do something about what is happening in your world, there will be no reinvention. There will be no change even though you might wish for it, talk about it, even complain about it. Your adapted strategies fueled by the ego voice will continue to run your life until someday you hit a wall and say, "Enough."

Reinvention cannot take place if you are not aware of how you feel, what you are doing, and what the consequences of your actions are. That's because reinvention is an inside job. You must open your mind to the journey at hand. When your mind is open, awareness comes with it, and with that comes the knowledge as to what step to take in the moment. Awareness is not the whole journey, but it is the first step, the beginning of reinvention.

The moving-on journey starts with acknowledging that the traumatic event actually happened. Most of us stay in denial for a while, not wanting to accept the reality of the situation. If we lose our job, the thing we know is to go and find a new job in the same field. However, with the market changes happening as fast as they are, we may have difficulties finding the type of work we know and begin to feel hopeless. After all, who wants someone with salt-and-pepper hair and thirty years of experience when there is so much young talent in the market? When we are in denial, we shut ourselves off to outside help because we think we can do it alone. When we move out of denial, we open up to the possibility that someone can help us. We live our lives as though nothing will ever change, using our adaptive strategies and behaviors to make the best of our day-to-day lives as we know them. As one of my clients told me, "I got lazy over twenty years with the company. I thought I would retire with them. It was a shock when they let me go."

You might ask, "Is there such a thing as reinvention? Can a

leopard change its spots? Do we ever really change deep down?" I don't think a leopard can change its spots, but I do think we can change on a deep level by becoming aware of and understanding the essential journey we have been on since birth and will continue to be on until we die. Yes, I think we can reinvent ourselves, both in our ways of acting and our ways of being. Perhaps the more important of the ways of being is your way of being with yourself. The relationship you have with yourself is what determines the relationship you have with the world.

As I have seen in my own experiences as well as those of my friends, clients, and colleagues, three particular areas of trauma lead to the opportunity for reinvention: ending of a significant relationship, job termination, and health issues. I know each of these traumas intimately, having been personally affected by all three.

We can take on reinvention from a position of inspiration or desperation. Unfortunately, it seems most of us need an event that forces us to look at our lives before we choose to reinvent ourselves. Even if the reinvention process is started through a difficult situation, we have the choice whether to take it on or not. Many times, we do not listen to or see what is going on, and as a result we repeat the same behaviors over and over again.

Reinvention is a time of renewal at the essential heart-and-soul level. It is an in-depth change that opens new vistas, new experiences, and new skills development at a time when we may least want those things.

Your Power to Choose

One of the most important, powerful, and positive aspects of being human is the power to choose. The power to choose is a fundamental element of your essential self that provides you with the ability to take on the challenge of walking a new path. This challenge can bring up lots of feelings, such as excitement, fear, and doubt. When reinvention is called for, you will either choose to take it on or choose to remain in the status quo.

Your brain has billions of neurons that send and receive signals to one another every nanosecond in an intricate web. All the experiences of your life are stored in these connections, creating a powerful library of information. When a situation arises that pushes you into a reinvention phase, your brain goes to work searching the database for information that will help you decide what to do. In any situation there are three possible reactions: flight, fight, or freeze. If fear is present, then information will be brought forward in an attempt to alleviate the fear. The options you have are based on the choices you make not only in this moment but also as you go on the journey of reinvention. Yes, the journey takes time. It is not done in a day, and it can be an exciting, fearful, exhilarating journey when you use your power of choice to screw up your courage and continue in the face of what looks like overwhelming odds. I just want you to know what your options are as you face reinvention of your life. All of us will face reinvention at some point because life is like that. It brings us experiences like waves in the ocean. They come in, and they go out. They are sometimes huge and sometimes small. Yet all of them are calling us to choose.

Questions to Consider

1. How did I adapt in my family?
2. What attitudes and beliefs did I learn in my family growing up?
3. What stories of my life do I still carry from childhood?
4. How do these stories not serve me anymore?
5. What choices am I making for my life?

Chapter 2

An Ending Is a Beginning

All human beings are self-aware, self-sensing and self-moving.
—Thomas Hanna

You might say the journey of reinvention is a hero's journey. Joseph Campbell is the one who first identified the idea of the hero's journey, and Christopher Vogler, a Hollywood executive, later adapted the idea into a twelve-stage hero's journey that he applied to movies such as *The Lion King*.

The Hero's Journey

The hero lives a busy life taken up by work and family mostly. Even though he feels his family, work, and friends are the safe place, the place of most comfort, he is, at a deeper level, feeling the disharmony in this life. He attempts to not disturb the balance of his life, yet forces are at work that will pull him away. Our hero would prefer to ignore these rumblings he feels but cannot identify, so he carries on.

This is the place most of us live most of the time. We were taught as children to establish our lives and our nests and do our best not to disturb them. However, this approach is a delusional way of living our lives because there are so many uncontrollable elements that might affect us. For example, in the summer of 2013, the flood of the century caused billions of dollars in damage in my city and the surrounding area. Thousands of people had to be evacuated, and some lost their homes forever due to damages beyond repair. This was a physically, emotionally, and intellectually challenging event in many people's lives. The journey to a new beginning was called for, and we had the opportunity to do it in a way in which we used our essential selves rather than our adapted selves. However, old habits die hard, and so millions of dollars have been spent trying to put everything back together the way it used to be. This is an apt metaphor for our lives. How many times have we tried to put things back the way they were when we knew in our hearts it would never happen? Trudy was in a nineteen-year marriage. She said she knew when she walked down the aisle she should not marry this man. She worked on it for all those years trying to fix what could not be fixed. Adaptations we learned when we less than eight years old can still be at work when we are forty years old. This is the call for you to take the hero's journey that almost everyone wants to deny, at least in the moment. Still the time has come for you, the hero, to leave the comfortable place and start on the journey.

Thomas Hanna, who invented the somatic method of healing, wrote extensively about how the brain-body connection is affected by trauma. Since childhood we have been subjected to various kinds of stress from the outside world, such as family or career, all of which have created certain neural connections in our brains that allow us to function at a particular level and in a particular way. However, we are a long way from our optimal operating mode—our essential selves. You must depart on the journey called for, using the tools and skills you know at that moment. The exciting possibility is that you will learn new skills and open the brain-body connection in ways that will bring you closer to knowing your essential self. You have the chance to uncover a more pure and powerful self that has been waiting to be brought into the light.

Essential Journey—A Journey of Thriving

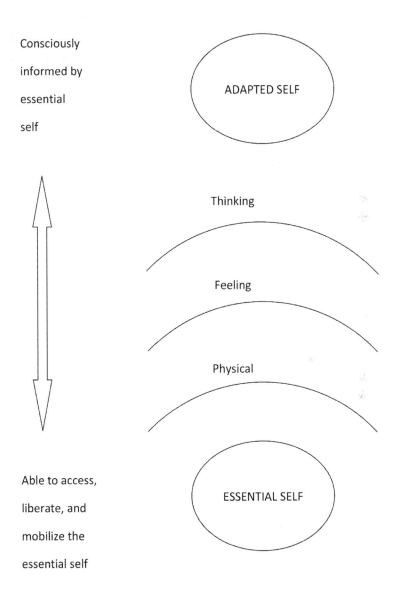

Consciously informed by essential self

ADAPTED SELF

Thinking

Feeling

Physical

Able to access, liberate, and mobilize the essential self

ESSENTIAL SELF

The first step of the journey is choice. Even though you don't know the full extent of the journey, you must choose it in order to jump-start your brain into action. When something cracks your heart open, you have the opportunity to open your heart and mind to what has happened and redirect your life to new possibilities. It is through this opening to the voice of your heart that possibilities arise. One of my clients was going through a difficult divorce. She was married for twenty-three years to an alcoholic who became abusive when he drank. She lived in fear of her and her children's safety. She felt that all of her self-esteem had been stripped away, leaving her a shell of her former self. The adapted self has a loud voice because that is the part of us we rely on most of the time to make our life choices. In this case my client realized she had to look deeply into her heart for the courage to move out of the family home and make way for her own life. When we are stripped to the core, the only part of us available is our essential selves. The essential self has a soft voice, so we must take quiet time to listen to it.

In this journey you get to choose which information and guidance you receive from others is right for you. You need to be present to discern for yourself what path you want to take, not the path someone else says you need to take. This is like research, where you go looking for people to talk to in the search for what you should do next. Sometimes the thing that is called for is just silence. Sit in silence listening to the beating of your heart and your breath going in and out, and become aware of what it is within you that will guide you.

Reinvention calls for faith in yourself. On the surface this may seem a simple principle, yet it is very important. Your journey will be fraught with danger if you give your trust away to someone or something else as though he, she, or it has the power and you don't. A friend of mine recently told me at a coffee meeting that he had received some bad news from his doctor. His tests had indicated that he was one step away from cancer of the bladder. My friend reported the findings as though he already had cancer. This is an example of a powerful source telling us something that takes us down the rabbit hole of planning for our demise. My friend did *not* have cancer, and he needed to get back to his own guidance as to what he needed to do about his health. He had given his life away and put it in the hands of his doctor when what was called for was to stay in his own power. In order to face the challenges that come with reinvention, you will need to learn to trust yourself. How do you develop this skill? Perhaps you think that you always make the wrong choices. First, you have to believe you have a strong intuition that will always guide you. You just haven't used it much, so you need to dust it off and wake it up by listening to the voice of your heart, which will manifest as a gut feel. You have experienced this kind of gut feeling at some time in your life. Take some time to remember when your gut told you the way to go. You might have last used your intuition when you were much younger, but it has always been there.

Potholes or Not ...

Your mind will raise all the doubts it can as it evaluates the circumstances and chooses options for you to follow. Many of these doubts will be based on fear of failure or habits and ways of being you learned along ago. As my father used to say, "Don't take a road you don't know, son. There are too many potholes you may fall into." He was a man who feared the road unknown. We take these attitudes and behaviors from our parents, make them our own, and proceed into adulthood without examining their usefulness to us. However, here we are on the reinvention journey, and potholes or not we are pushed to step forward into the unknown. Your adapted behaviors and beliefs will scream at you not to take what looks like a dangerous journey. You can courageously face these doubts and fears with the awareness that the stories you learned as a child do not serve you anymore. On this journey you will dive deep into the truth of who you are, looking for your essential self. There is a strong element of awareness at this point. You will realize you have been acting in ways that are counterproductive to what you want in life. You will ask questions such as, "Where am I?" and "Who am I?" These are important questions to answer so you can start to develop a new perspective on the qualities you have and what you value most in the world.

I want to tell you about Ray, a friend of mine who loves to work with people. Ray had a story about himself brought forward from childhood that everyone was better than him and that conflict should be avoided at all costs. Despite this damaging adapted mind-set, for over eighteen years he did well in his career. He respected and supported his staff and provided as much training as he could in order to give them the tools for advancement. Then he got a new boss. The new boss was housed in the head office thousands of miles away from where Ray worked, so they met by phone, not in person. Qualifications are so often held out as sacred, most especially in the tech industry. This new boss had the MBA and technical qualifications to get him to the top of the company division, and he let Ray know it in no uncertain terms. Ray, on the other hand, had a natural gift of working with people but had not done much upgrading over his career in terms of technical qualifications. As Ray listened to the qualifications of his new boss and the goals that had been set, fear set in. His heart rate elevated, and he began to sweat. The story of "He is better than me" echoed in his head as though it were being amplified by a speaker system. He also made the assumption, based again on his history, that the new boss did not like him or understand him. Ray was suffering from sensory emotional amnesia. He had buried his connection to his essential self and become so habituated in the story of others being better than him that he lived his life from this perspective.

We all have these stories of our lives that we learned long ago in childhood, and though the events that initiated the story are long forgotten, we continue to live the stories in the present moment as though they are true. Thomas Hanna, the founder of somatics, says it is a good thing that sensory amnesia is a learned behavior, as it means it can be unlearned.

Six months after the new boss was hired, Ray was fired. Ray had tried to make the new relationship work based on his old behaviors. One of his habits was, unfortunately, to not keep his boss fully informed of what he was doing, the goals that had been set and accomplished, and how much his team respected him. Ray had taken a group of six people living in different countries and working in a virtual environment and created a community of people who shared ideas, goals, and innovations. He had accomplished most of this prior to the new boss showing up, and he did not have the confidence or awareness to bring this information forward. He had learned that polite people did not blow their own horn. His fear of conflict and feeling intimidated by someone presumed to be better than him prevented him from asking important questions of his new boss that might have opened the door to discovering how the relationship could work ... or not. Ray could have given himself the opportunity for clarity. He could have requested the two of them meet to clearly lay out the goals and expectations for the future. When I asked him why he did not make an appointment to meet face-to-face with his new boss in San Diego, Ray said, "I never thought I could do that."

When you understand who you are, you are able to access the wisdom, courage, and determination that you need for this journey. You must dig deep inside yourself to find your essential self that will not let you quit even in the face of fear and what looks like impossible odds. This is where the power lies. It is within you, not with someone or something else over which you have no control.

I now know this for myself, but I wasn't so aware of where my power lay when I faced significant health issues in my fifties. My wife had just been honored with the Woman of Vision award for our city and was being interviewed at our home by a television reporter. My phone rang in the middle of the interview, and I took the call in another room. My doctor told me to come into his office as soon as possible. My gut tightened. Having gone through a battery of tests in the previous three months, I knew I had cancer.

The confirmed diagnosis took me on a journey of more testing, crying, talking, researching various options, and feeling powerless. I had this mass growing in my abdomen over which I had no control. Given my history of shutting down my emotions in the face of adversity, I once again turned inward to isolation. In somatic terminology this is called the red-light response, which is when the body collapses into itself toward a fetal position for protection. If this position is held for a long time, the body will develop an inward curvature and forget how to stand tall. This is sensory motor amnesia, a condition in which the body-brain feedback loop gets stuck in a particular pattern and the body literally cannot stand up straight. Although my wife was supportive, I felt alone. I felt angry and hard done by. "Why me?" I shouted. I fought the diagnosis in my mind. I did not want cancer. I did not feel like I had the guts to fight it. I did not want to go on this hero's journey. The fear of the unknown is a step in the hero's journey where the hero tries to push away the call to move out of his or her ordinary life. I went into despair. I felt I was being punished for the life I had led up until then.

The process from diagnosis to medical intervention is a long one. After testing of various sorts over a period of five months, I was given an appointment with a surgeon. He said I had a choice to have the intricate and invasive surgery within a week, in the latter part of September, or wait at least six months. My daughter was engaged, and her wedding was coming up soon. I had to make a decision. If I waited, the chances were the tumor would grow significantly and possibly spread throughout my body, which was like imagining an army of bugs flooding my system with poison for which I had no antidote. There were two fears barking within me—the fear I would die if I waited and the fear of the invasive surgery, which potentially could lead to permanent damage. The choice may seem simple, yet fear is powerful and not necessarily logical. I chose to have the surgery within the week, and since then, I've lived with the consequences of nerve damage.

In cases of challenging experiences the red-light reaction of the mind and body is a natural response and serves us well in the short run. However, the hero is called to take this journey into the unknown danger and still forge ahead. My physical, thinking, and feeling natures collapsed within me as I fought to deny the reality of the cancer diagnosis. Once again the context for my life had dissipated, and I felt as if there was no way to move forward. The feeling of being powerless was an old one for me. It left me frozen and isolated.

At this point I had no thought of reinvention. I was now fully engaged in the medical system, trying to determine if there was a next step for me within the limited options of this system. My thought process was about survival. Sometimes the journey starts out like this, and once we embrace survival, then we can make a choice about how we will move forward. The active ingredient is choice. It is through our power of choice that we can embark on the journey of reinvention even though the journey looks fearful and dangerous.

I knew I had to live. I had more to do in my life still; I couldn't die at fifty-six. All of us have the knowing to follow the impulses given to us. It just may not be turned on. However, through a traumatic event, the heart cracks open, and we have the opportunity to look and listen to what is inside. We shift our perspective from outside in to inside out. There is a huge sense of loss and powerlessness in a cancer diagnosis and in any trauma. But we are not powerless. No matter what the situation, we can choose how to react. We have the ability to look from the inside out and know how we feel, and we can connect the brain-body feedback loop to help us through our journey. No matter the extent of the injury, *we* decide how we will undertake the journey. My daughter was being married in a few months, and I was determined to walk her down the aisle. Rather than choose death, I chose life because I had something to live for.

She was my light in a dark tunnel. If she had not been in my life at that time, I might have chosen a different path. When we have a purpose, we have a reason to take the hero's journey.

Letting Go of Control

Planning, organizing, and controlling circumstances were hallmarks in my family. Surely it was possible to control life's circumstances, I thought. Learning to let go of control has been a lifelong endeavor for me. We humans have learned to hold on to the old ways. These adapted behaviors are habitual ways of being that we learned when we were young and taking in huge amounts of information as to how life works. The more we struggle to hold on to the old ways, the more they stick with us and have us make decisions from an old paradigm. Like getting gum off your shoe, reinventing your life based on your ability to self-sense, self-motivate, and self-choose takes specific and repetitive practice. You work to clean off the old gum so your shoes don't stick to the floor, and you keep cleaning the gum off until your shoes are clean.

At the point I let go of how the process would unfold, and I made a choice to live. No matter how the surgery went, I would live my life to the best of my ability and awareness. To this day I live with the aftereffects of my experience with cancer. Although cancer is never forgotten, I live my life with gratitude for my health and awareness of my emotions.

The process of reinvention is a daily practice, meaning the techniques of meditation, mindfulness, and awareness, which I will teach you later, should be applied to your life every day. Each I acknowledge the skills I have learned, like not stuffing my emotions anymore, and let go of beating myself up for sometimes falling back into old habits, like isolating when I feel afraid. The reinvention process is like washing a shirt with stains on it. You spot clean the dirty, greasy spots before you wash the shirt. Then when it comes out, it is mostly clean with just a few minor spots left. I allow myself to be pleased with what I have accomplished, such as bringing kindness and self-compassion to myself during the day, because reinvention is a daily process done over time. For example, I have made it a practice to go to yoga five days a week for the quiet, focused time and the opportunity to stretch my body in ways that are nurturing to me. I still have areas needing improvement, which is the daily hero's journey, such as noticing when I have disconnected my heart from my surroundings.

Transforming your life through reinvention is a nonlinear process. A geophysicist described it like melting snow. The snow warms up underneath the surface, but you cannot see it melting. The snow accumulates warmth over time, and all of a sudden the snow disappears in a day. The process then speeds up, as melting begets melting. It takes a lot of energy to change from one path to another, yet it is possible and exciting to do so by making a choice, fostering awareness, and engaging in regular practice. The more we change and move along our path of reinvention, the more aware we become. This gives us the confidence to keep going.

Questions to Consider

1. Who am I?
2. Where am I?
3. What do I have to live for?
4. What is unique about me?
5. What is it time to let go of?

Chapter 3

Neuroscience and the Hero's Journey

We are always in a perpetual state of being created and creating ourselves.

—Dan Siegel

Nothing happens in the body or in our feeling or thinking selves without a message from the brain. The growing scientific field of neuroscience provides important information for us on our journeys. The connection between our brains, our physiologies, and our psychologies is of great importance in understanding our journeys and the personal control we have over how we take those journeys on.

First, my disclaimer, I am not a scientist. However, I've read the amazing literature and studies about the capabilities of our brains and how we can use this information to better live our lives. The reinvention journey relies on an understanding of your brain's abilities and the wonderful possibilities of your life when the information is applied to your circumstances.

Our Plastic Brains

Your brain is completely plastic. It changes constantly as you use it, and the ability to change the neural connections in your brain never decreases as you get older.

Our brains weigh only about three pounds or 2 percent of our body weight, yet they are powerhouses of activity with over one hundred billion neurons. The neurons are the basic working units of the brain and connect with other neurons in unique ways.

Without going into all the science, just look at the brain like a huge series of electrical connections firing in various sequences. Imagine a forest of trees where each tree has thousands of tiny endings that are equipped to fire off electrical signals to the other tress in the forest. Every electrical impulse goes exactly to the right tree to complete the task being requested. If you hurt your hand, for example, certain neurons will fire to accentuate the pain, and others will fire to tell you what you need to do about alleviating the pain. The correct trees in the forest have connected through these electrical impulses to provide the pain response and the thought process for alleviating the pain.

Over time the neurons create patterns of activity. Certain repeated activity have the neurons firing in the same sequence over and over. Each child develops certain neural firing patterns, creating habits of activity as well as feeling and thinking patterns that become hallmarks of how the child lives his or her life unless he or she learns how to change the pattern. For example, a mother's particular way of responding to her child will teach the child how to get the response he or she wants in life in order to fulfill a desire, such as getting fed. Over time this way of acting in the world becomes second nature as the child carries forward ways of acting to get what he or she wants.

Habits are formed when we do things over and over. These habits have neural firing patterns associated with them. You might say, "I'm hardwired this way. This is how I am." It might look and feel like you are hardwired in a certain way when in fact your habitual pattern has been learned and is simply a bunch of neurons firing in a particular sequence.

The downside of these habitual patterns is they become automatic. We live from them without thinking because they are stimulated by external events. The feedback loop from the brain to the nervous system and then to our psychological or physical selves has locked itself into a hardened pattern. This pattern has to be disrupted in order for us to take the hero's journey and have a successful reinvention.

The good and powerful news is that we can change our neural firing sequences through choice and practice.

Choosing the Journey

Choice is the starting point. You must choose this hero's journey even though you do not know every step of the way. The fear in you will rise along with the bile in your throat, and still you must make the choice in order to reinvent your life.

To change our neural firing patterns we need to become conscious and aware. By learning specific skills—like intentionality, working with awareness every day, and other skills detailed in this book—we will begin to experience changes.

Changing Old Patterns

In his book *The Life We Are Given* (1995), Michael Murphy outlines the transformations experienced by two groups over about one year, demonstrating that old patterns can be changed. When Murphy wrote the book, he did not have the scientific evidence we have today, but he was on the leading edge of what has since become a wealth of information about how the brain works, how neurons connect with one another, and how neural firing patterns can be changed through specific practice. Still science is just at the tip of the knowledge base when it comes to the brain's working mechanisms.

The brain is a complex organ that has more than one hundred billion connections. The number of neural firings in one minute is almost beyond our comprehension. Yet the system works in a brilliant way, allowing us to process all the visual, auditory, and sensory information around us in radically fast fashion.

I do not intend to provide a detailed description of how the brain works and all the implications for your actions. However, it is important to have a basic understanding of how the brain works, as it demonstrates the power each of us has to change the electrical connections in our brains to give us different results than in the past. Old habits die hard, but we have the power to change them by understanding the physical and mental ways to do so. You will be surprised by the changes that will occur in your life when you use the tools described in this book in a dedicated practice that leads to a new you.

In his book *Mindsight: The New Science of Personal Transformation*, Dr. Dan Siegel describes how external events activate different regions of the brain, which then give us signals that push us to react in a certain way. For example, all of us have heard of the fight-flight-or-freeze response to events. Siegel describes this as originating in the brain stem, the oldest part of the brain. This region appears to be responsible for how we respond to life-threatening or scary events. This region also regulates our feelings of satiation, as for food, shelter, and reproduction.

Siegel says that when we feel a deep drive for something, the brain stem is most likely operating in concert with the limbic area. The limbic area, also known as the mammalian brain, came to being more than two hundred million years ago. It works with the brain stem to control not only our basic drives but also our emotions. Siegel writes that the key question is, Is this good or bad? We move toward the good and away from the bad. Neural connections are firing all the time as we evaluate our next move.

This is why a mindful approach, a present-moment awareness, is so important to reinvention. The more aware you are of where you are in the process moment to moment, the better you can understand your response to events.

Want to stop smoking? Want to quit chewing your nails? Your brain will help you to change any habit. All you need to do is practice the skills I lay out in this book. The malleability of your brain is such that you actually change the physical makeup of your brain as you take on consciously different thinking patterns.

Two other parts of the brain that Siegel writes about are the amygdala, which is responsible for perceiving emotions such as sadness and anger, and the hippocampus, which stores emotional responses to various events so that the emotions may be recalled when similar events take place. The hippocampus is the part that pulls together pieces of information and emotion from other parts of the brain to create memories. Siegel refers to it as the "puzzle-piece-assembler." The ability to recall experiences from long ago is an important function because those experiences form the basis of present thought, evaluation, and decision making and thus determine the ways in which we act.

The various parts of the brain, including the brain stem, work together in an awe-inspiring way that allows us to function, react, and remember events and experiences. However, because of how the brain works, we sometimes develop sensory emotional amnesia, reacting to events in our adult lives in a similar way to how we reacted to events in our childhoods. Thankfully we have the tools and the means to change this behavior. Simply put, what has been learned can be unlearned.

The neocortex is considered the new part of the brain. It allows us to think and evaluate information and to form thinking patterns about subjects. The whole thing is a very complex set of firing neurons and stored connections that allows us to go about our lives on a daily basis.

The frontal lobe of the brain is where the executive function is situated. We make decisions and plans from here, deciding what the best course of action is at any moment in time. Scientists have shown that this part of the brain actually physically changes when we meditate.

The most important thing to remember is the brain is a malleable part of us that can change constantly with specific instructions from us. Changes in brain function can take place consciously or unconsciously depending on choices we make and actions we take. The brain loves to be taught new skills, with repetition being a key to changing neural patterns. The preferred method of changing your brain is to do so consciously because then you know what results you want and how to achieve those results. The ability to change never diminishes over our lives; it is always available to us. So whenever you want to change, no matter your age, you can do it. How great is that?

Your reinvention process is in your hands. You have the power and the means to change your life. You simply need to consciously choose a new way of living your life, and then your brain can be engaged on the journey with you.

Where does the mind fit in this picture? Dan Siegel says, "I believe (and cannot find any science to disprove) that an important aspect of the mind can be defined as an embodied and relational, emergent self-organizing process that regulates the flow of energy and information both within us and between and among us."

The self is not only embodied. It is also relational. We are relational beings. Our minds process and regulate the flow of energy and information within us and between us. This powerfully shows our connection to others in the world. Therefore, we can not only look outside ourselves for information and to learn from others but also use our self-sensing to look on the inside and know intuitively what we need and want.

This speaks to the idea of passion. If you are passionate about a certain subject, you can use what you know for the benefit of the world, not only those close around you. Then there is a sharing of knowledge on a local as well as broader stage of the world. When we are thrown into a state of reinvention through trauma, we are given the opportunity to look for our own knowing of who we are, what we want, and how we can use what we know to contribute to society.

Moving Forward

All this talk of change is not to say what we have done in the past has not been of value. We are simply looking at what is possible for our lives going forward from here. The lesson is we are totally capable of changing direction at any time. We may have had a particular career for many years, but we can start a new one right here and right now. We have the power, knowledge, experience, and energy to do that.

Patience is called for as you move along your new path, but do not waver from what you are learning in this new arena. You will uncover many gifts that you can then offer to yourself and the world as you are called upon to look with new eyes, to hear with new ears, and to feel with a sensitivity you are not used to. The great intellectual prowess you have been given now will work side by side with your emotional capacity to bring something new to you and then your world.

Questions to Consider

1. What ways of behaving do I want to change?
2. What evidence do I have that my brain is able to change neural patterns?
3. What have I always wanted to do that I have not done yet?

Chapter 4

Courage, Determination, and Patience

Before I can tell my life what I want to do with it, I must listen to my life telling me who I am.

—Parker J. Palmer

Present-moment awareness or mindfulness is a useful concept to learn when you are reinventing yourself. One description of mindfulness is the art of being aware. When we are mindful, we are awake to what is happening and feel our feet on the ground as we go about our activities.

Listen to Your Life

The reinvention journey requires courage, determination, and patience. When you learn to be present in the moment, you feel alive in the process. Nothing goes missing, including your feelings, what you say, and how you act. You become and stay fully aware of the things in your life you need to do first in this moment. What is the most important thing you can do right now? With this awareness you can take yourself to hopeful highs as the journey progresses.

One of my clients worked in a large corporation and had an income of over $20,000 per month, which led to a corresponding lifestyle. Then he was unceremoniously let go from his job without a final conversation or particular reason. He was left to make up the closing conversation in his mind. The devastation he felt was deep and raw.

The *New York Times* best-selling author Wayne Dyer would say, "Congratulations!" The universe or divine guidance or whatever name you have for it was giving him a message to move. It was time to find out what he was passionate about and go in that direction.

Passion

We are not well trained to know our passions. We have spent our lives working long and hard to reach the tops of our professions, and while we may say we love our jobs, they may not be our passions. For example, my client's passions were helping young entrepreneurs starting in business and having the intimacy of working one-on-one with people or with small groups. However, he had never had the chance to follow these passions because of the responsibilities required of him in the corporation.

Passion is like a shy rabbit in the forest that needs to be nurtured and encouraged to show up as we do our work to melt away the adaptations we have lived with all our lives. Each of us in our own unique way learned to act in a certain way to adapt to family and cultural circumstances. Even though we learned these adapted behaviors as children, we tend to repeat a version of them as adults and live from the paradigms we were taught. These adapted behaviors are challenging to notice and more challenging to change because our old systems love to keep things the way they are. The more we fight our adapted behaviors, the more they seem to entrench in our ways of behaving. So we need to accept them and love them and change them gradually.

Passion comes from the heart not the head. It is something that blossoms within you and makes itself known. Each of us has the capacity to listen to the voice of our heart. It is intuitive, intelligent guidance available to us all the time.

In my own experience, as I look back at my life and the way I lived and worked, I see that teaching was my passion. Unfortunately teaching was not always called for. At one point in my life I was a financial adviser selling insurance products. One day my manager took me aside and told me I needed to change the way I related to my prospective clients. I had no idea what he was talking about. He said I was trying to make my clients my friends by giving them loads of information. My strategy was to have them buy out of friendship rather than based on selling expertise. He said if a client asked me what time it was, I would explain how the watch was made. It was a slap in the face and a wake-up call to how I was out of sync with the selling process and was acting out of my adapted behaviors to avoid any bad feelings. Making my clients my friends was my adapted way of wanting to be loved. Adapted behaviors play a powerful role in our adult lives. Most of the time they are unconscious, as they were in my selling process. However, once we become conscious of them, we can change the neural patterns holding them in place.

Discovering your passion is one of the possible positive outcomes when you take the hero's journey. When you are in the thick of the reinvention process, you must let go of your ego, and you come face-to-face with your own truth. In this place your intuitive voice becomes clearer and clearer.

Intuition

Your intuition will always inform you of your path if you are listening. The voice of intuition is not loud and brash; it is subtle and one you may not be used to hearing. You need to be aware enough to receive the information. The tools described later in this book will help you open your ears to hear the soft voice of intuition.

It once took three separate but similar events over three years for my intuition to get my attention. The lesson here is that if you don't get it the first time and change direction, then the intuitive power at work will bring you more and more-serious lessons. It seems that when we are ready, the teacher shows up to try to move us out of our old place, our old way of doing things.

The first event occurred on a beautiful, sunny day in May. I was not paying attention while riding my bicycle, and I hit a guardrail. I flew off my seat and fell onto the handlebars of the bike, breaking two of my ribs. *No big deal,* I thought. *I will carry on.* I always saw one of my outstanding characteristics as determination. The harder things got, the harder I worked. Quit? Not me!

The next year, in May, I was walking my dogs at night, and a neighbor's dog attacked mine at exactly the moment I was beside a two-foot hollow on the walking path. One leg went into the hollow, and the other leg stayed on top, resulting in a spiral fracture of my left ankle. My neighbor was apologetic as I lay on the ground and moaned in pain. He took my dogs home and got my wife to call an ambulance.

Okay, this injury was a bit more serious. The ambulance showed up and took me to the hospital. The paramedic asked me if I'd ever had morphine. I said no. "Well," he said, "soon you will feel really good, and the pain will be gone." Five days later, my ankle had been rebuilt with five pins to hold it together, and a large cast held everything in place for eight weeks. Still I did not hear the call for a life-changing process. I saw the injury as a physical challenge to learn how to make coffee while balancing on crutches. You might think I would get the message that I needed to look at my life, how I was living it, but not a chance. I thought my life was going great with the new partnership my wife and I had. The tougher things got, the more I buckled down to get the job done. That was the rule I lived by. I didn't know another way.

If you don't listen the first time, the message will be stronger the second time, and if you don't listen the second time, then you can expect a dramatic turn of events that will stop you in your tracks.

Sure enough, a year later, once again in May, my doctor called to tell me I had prostate cancer. As I described earlier, I had radical surgery in September. When you have a major illness, various medical specialists poke and prod and exam your body over and over again. By the time I was done, there was not an inch of my body inside or out that some doctor or nurse had not examined. When I was taken into the surgical suite, the nurse asked if I knew why I was there. I think they ask this to make sure they have the right patient for the right operation. I told her, and I asked her to tell everyone there to be at their best that day. I will never forget her saying, "Don't worry; God will be here too."

When we are faced with trauma, we become children again. Our essential selves rise up and help us go forward. The ego slips into the background, and we are in touch with the essential part of us again. My essential self was fully present after my surgery. I felt as though I was connected to my world from the inside out. My actions and decisions came from my intuitive nature rather than my intellect and ego. It was a time of peace in my life. The ego, however, is a powerful part of us developed to help us get along in the world. After a few years, I was once again operating my life from my ego. This is the part of the hero's journey where obstacles are placed in our path. Since I remembered what it was like to live from my essential self, I had the knowledge to open to my heart again and practice living from my essential self.

As we embark on the hero's journey to reinvent our lives, we must learn how to reengage from time to time to live from the inside out on a daily basis. The awareness that your renewed way of living can be different from your past is a practice that we need daily to be successful in reinvention. In a gentle yet effective way, as you enhance your awareness of everyday living, you can move forward in the face of fear and doubt.

The Life-Giving Cycle

Reinvention is possible, and the opportunity may come at the oddest of times, as you can see from my own physically traumatic experiences. At the same time it is one of the best journeys you will take in your life.

The ending of anything also announces the beginning of something new. When you take this journey, you open your life to acceptance of how things were and an acceptance of your life as you want it to be. There is a five-step process of facing the ending of the old way in order to start the journey of reinvention: denial, anger, sorrow, self-compassion, and acceptance. This is the life-giving cycle, for without acknowledging the losses and the deep changes we cannot open ourselves to what is new.

Denial

The state of denial is a natural place to go in the short term. It's a place where we say things like "This is a minor setback. I'll be up and running soon." Perhaps we don't talk to anyone about what is happening. We rationalize what is taking place, convincing ourselves that it is just a phase and will pass. In this stage of the journey we want things to remain as they were and have not accepted yet that a phase of our lives is done. The ending of a significant relationship, a job loss, and health issues are not passing phases. They signify the closing of a chapter in our lives.

Denial is a temporary phase if you wake up to the reality of the situation. Although it can be a helpful phase in the short run, to live in denial for a long time will harm you more than help. Do you know someone who lives in denial? How much happiness and fulfillment do they have? I expect not much. At some point, we realize we must move on through the life-giving journey to the next step: anger.

Anger

Not many of us like to feel anger. Some people refuse to get angry because they saw the negative consequences of out-of-control anger in past family experiences. Others do not know how to express anger because they never saw it in their families. I had no experience of anger growing up, so I had no skill in expressing it when I faced circumstances in which it was a legitimate emotion. Some people are afraid to express anger because of their fear of reprisal.

Anger is not a bad thing when expressed in a healthy way, and left unexpressed, it will turn inward and hurt you. How does anger help us? It is an emotion with energy, so it helps us to get things done.

You may know someone who holds anger close to his or her heart and lives from that place. People who live this way have nothing good to say about people, especially those they feel have wronged them. How often do you want to be with these people? My guess would be not very often.

What is the first emotion babies express when they are born? Anger! Someone slaps them on the bottom, and they wail and scream as though they are in the wrong place. They have been taken from a warm, nourishing place where they were taken care of and thrust into a harsh environment in which they have to adapt or die. It makes them angry. It was time for birth, though. It was time to up the ante of their lives and start living in the experience of being fully human. It was time to reinvent themselves from living in the womb to living in the outside world.

When we are called to reinvent our lives, we are similar to newborn babies. We must move from a comfortable place and start living from a new place. Our anger is justified, but it does not change the fact that our lives are now on a new track. Like babies, we must take in the breath of life or suffer the consequences.

Sorrow

Sorrow is a place on the journey very few of us relish visiting. Most of us would rather avoid sorrow because we fear depression and long-lasting bad feelings.

Sorrow is a legitimate feeling that is to be moved through rather than lived with. Once the past has been acknowledged as it was, we face the task of working through our sorrow over the loss.

The loss of a relationship, a job, our health, or whatever is best acknowledged and released. We cannot make progress on the path of reinvention if we hold on to the sorrow of what used to be. Even though the past was an important part of our lives, it cannot be recovered, and if truth be known, we may not want to recover it. Sorrow is released a little bit at a time. We can ease sorrow through tears, which are a release of pain, and by speaking to someone we trust to clear the rubble of the past. In many cases writing a letter of good-bye is a helpful technique. You write a letter saying good-bye to all the good, bad, and delusional things about the past, and then you use a ritual such as burning it to say a final good-bye. Another technique you can use is to set a timer for ten or twenty minutes and write about the experience. Get your feelings out on paper, and when the time is up, get rid of the writing. This may be done over several days or longer. Eventually, the sorrow will dissipate.

Maybe the past was not as good as you thought it was. Perhaps your ego made up a story for you to rationalize what looked like a good thing but was really bad for you. Acknowledge your sorrow, and move through it. Do not hold on to it. This part of the journey is an important time for personal work to clear the wreckage of the past. I often recommend to clients that they take the time to journal their stories, not only the bad but also the good, and what they have learned along the way. This is a great way to sharpen your awareness of who you are and what you bring with you into your life now.

Many times I have worked with clients who have been through a divorce, health crisis, or career loss and carry the baggage of the past with them by living as though the traumatic event happened yesterday. When you live in the past in the delusional hope that past circumstances were different, you tie yourself to a stake in the ground, just like a circus elephant being trained. When you do this, you have nowhere to go. You must let go and start with a clean slate to move on to the next chapter of your life. Resistance to what is being shown to you is futile and a waste of your life energy.

How can you let go of what you feel is unjust or hurtful? You let go through forgiveness. Lily Tomlin said, "Forgiveness means giving up all hope of a better past."

"How," you may ask, "can I forgive someone who has unjustly hurt me?" You start with yourself. You forgive that which you did not see, did not respond to, or did not participate in. You let yourself off the hook from self-blame, self-criticism, and self-hate by treating yourself with compassion. You treat yourself the same way you would treat a good friend who is hurting from a negative experience.

Self-Compassion

Self-compassion is not something many of us know much about. We learned how the world works according to our parents and have mostly followed their way of being in the world. Many of us know the voice of self-criticism, though. Perceived failure leads to a chastising voice about how we could have and should have done better. We falsely believe that poor performance requires a punishment to get us back on track. After all, if we could have done better, then why didn't we? This criticizing voice was perhaps once the voice of our parents and now has become our own voice.

Kristin Neff writes in her book, *Self-Compassion*, that we must acknowledge our own suffering. She says that we live in a society that has developed a culture of criticism and self-judgment.

We need to learn to treat ourselves as we would a good friend who is having a difficult time. We would bring them compassion and understanding, and this compassionate understanding is what we must also bring ourselves.

The voice of self-compassion sounds something like this: "May I be loving to myself. May I forgive myself. May I appreciate myself for who I am. May I be kind to myself. May I be grateful for my life."

Self-compassion is not a one-shot deal. We must practice it one day at a time and allow for the flow of self-love to arise within us. In this way we let go of the old and move toward the new.

Acceptance

The last step in opening to a new way is acceptance. In this step we start to plan our new lives without reference to the old ways. We make plans, even if they are simple ones, to start something new for ourselves. Perhaps we take time to look back in our lives and see what it is we loved at one time that we have forgotten.

A friend of mine, Darina, was a representative of a pharmaceutical company in Ireland and traveled all over the country. Many days she was away from home. For ten years she traveled and represented her firm respectably, but this kind of life was hard. Then her father-in-law passed away, and he left his farm to his son John, Darina's husband. It was a poor man's farm to say the least, but John loved the farming life.

Darina realized that with the passing of her father-in-law she was being led on a journey to a new life. Although she did not know what the path looked like, she was willing to take the journey of reinvention.

This adventurous couple took over the farm and got to work. In addition to the main house on the property, there was an old house that John's dad used to rent out in the summer. Darina and John renovated the old house and started a bed-and-breakfast. The taste of success was sweet. Darina loved meeting the guests and offering them an authentic part of Ireland made real through her caring and welcoming ways. One thing led to another, and single-handedly they added a huge wing to their own home, creating more rooms for weary travelers. They embraced reinvention with hard work, courage, and persistence. Every traveler who has the good fortune to stay with them feels the love and acceptance they bring to every encounter.

Darina's reinvention took hard work, but mostly it took an acceptance of what was being shown to her. Her acceptance and decision to follow the path that was shown to her led her to a reinvention she never would have thought of on her own. That is the kind of reinvention possible when you pay attention to what is being shown to you and then take action.

What is being shown to you in your life? Are you afraid to move in a new direction? When you stop, let go, and listen, you will be guided to see what is possible. I am reinventing myself through writing books. I used to be a corporate executive and then became a life coach, and now I am moving into another reinvention of what I consider to be my full expression. What is yours? Don't shy away from it.

Questions to Consider

1. What is the ongoing voice of my ego?
2. How can I be more self-compassionate?
3. What or whom do I need to forgive?
4. What is my passion?
5. Can I reinvent my life?

Chapter 5

Doubt Is in the Air

Crisis is the way the universe pushes us to move on.
—Julio Olalla, former Chilean government lawyer and life coach

You and I are heroes in our own right. We have lives to live, yet time passes so quickly. A friend of mine with a fourteen-month-old baby told me she is trying to enjoy every moment with her daughter because she feels how fast the months have gone by. Soon the baby will be walking, talking, and playing with friends outside the house. How many time have we said to one another, "Where did the time go?"

I just celebrated thirty years of marriage with the most amazing woman. How did these years go so fast? I commented to my wife the other day how grateful I am that even today we can sit together and talk about our lives with a fresh perspective every day. Reinvention has become a habitual practice for me. I recognize that life is always evolving, and I now embrace these changes, not resist them. Since emotions were not a common element in my family of origin, I always had difficulty expressing my feelings. Now, every day I can check in and examine how I feel and express these feelings to my wife, notwithstanding my history of fear and doubt about letting people know how I feel. This is reinvention in action.

Doubts

Whenever we take on something new, we will have doubts that arise from our past experiences. We resist what we don't know or understand until we can grasp how it will affect our lives. These doubts play into the fact that the reinvention journey is not always clear. We must have the courage to take the first step. As we continue on the journey, we will gain confidence, and eventually, by practicing over and over again, we will create a new habitual way of living.

As we go forward, memories are triggered because our minds are conditioned to base decisions and actions on physical and emotional data that have been stored based on experiences. The mind has two ways to retrieve memories. One is recognition, and the other is recall. Recognition is a simple comparison of what was previously experienced—for example, comparing a particular type of dog previously encountered with a dog that is currently in front of you.

With recall, the mind has more difficulty bringing up an accurate picture because the sensory data have been stored in various parts of the brain. So the mind pulls together bits of information from different places to create a picture and feelings that it can apply to the current situation. Therefore the recall may not be an exact mirror image of what was previously experienced. So the data the mind pulls together from past experiences does not always apply well to the current situation, but we are not aware of this process unless we understand how the mind works, as described here.

Along these lines, since the path forward in the reinvention journey is not always clear, our brains trigger a fear response and try to keep us safe by bringing up doubts. These doubts come to us by way of the voice of the ego, which speaks loudly and with authority. It is a very familiar voice. It used to be the voice of our parents, and over time we made it our own while retaining their biases. We are prone to follow this voice because what it suggests may seem like the safest route. For example, when faced with this unknown path, you may feel physical discomfort, like a knot in your stomach, due to fear. Your ego then tells you to stop, to not take the next step in this perilous journey. Nothing appears certain in this path, so the ego loves to argue against undertaking the journey by providing an ongoing dialogue devoted to certainty: "Why are you doing this? Don't do this; it isn't safe. You remember back when? You are never going to make it. You have failed more than once trying it this way. Don't do it again. You're too old now. Don't try that. Shame on you. You should have done better." And on and on.

Your ego never gives up trying to keep you in the old pattern so you can have the old feeling of being safe. It provides a running commentary on your life in every moment, directing you to take certain actions based on its experience of your past. The more you listen and believe it, the more you are trapped in the cage of history, destined to repeat the events of the past.

Doubt, fear, and worry are constructs of the mind that are available to us for good reason. If a bear is attacking you in the woods, you best be fearful of the outcome. However, doubt, fear, and worry will hold you back from taking the hero's journey to a reinvented life that is based on knowing your truth rather than continuing to act out of your old adapted habits.

Overcoming Doubts

Reinvention is a path that can be exhilarating and exciting and open new vistas to your life never previously imagined. However, nothing will appear certain at the beginning of the journey. You will have to learn to trust yourself and let your intuitive nature guide you.

Doubt needs to be faced head on, not with a heavy hand but with an accepting heart. Doubt is part of who you are. It has your past down pat. It guides you to know how you should react to situations, even though your reactions are historically based.

Give it the courageous kick and say, "No, not this time." Early in my second marriage I was still drinking, which upset my new wife. I had little awareness of the effect my behavior had on our relationship. After two years of being together she finally sat me down and said she could not be with me any longer if I continued to drink. I really heard her, and I decided right then and there to stop drinking. I said no to the voice of my ego that said I did not have a drinking problem. I wanted my marriage more than I wanted to listen to the old voice. That decision changed my life forever.

Listen to the impulse of your heart to follow this new path with confidence. Thank the doubt for coming. It is trying to help you. Then stay the course by listening carefully to your heart and your intuition. Doubt is your friend, not your enemy. There is no need to disassociate from it. Just accept it as part of your process, then ask it to go to its room for a nap. You don't need it right now.

Questions to Consider

1. What do I doubt myself about?
2. What do I want to say no to today?
3. What is the ongoing picture I have of myself?

Chapter 6

Sensory Self Amnesia

Without awareness of how you respond to stress mentally, physically, and emotionally, you will undo your progress in no time at all.

—Martha Peterson

All of us are born with an essential self as part of our makeup. Some call it the truth of us. Some call it gut feel. You know this part of you. Through your life you have had experiences in which you absolutely knew you were doing the right thing and were on the right path. We were all declared miracles as babies. The miracle does not change when we grow up; we just put it in the back room and forget about it while we live from our adapted selves.

The Essential Self

The essential self is the part of you that lives life and thrives. There is an impulse within the essential self that is life itself. The essential self is the truth of who you are. It is a knowing deep within you that you can trust to guide you. Unfortunately, we move away from our essential selves as we adapt to survive in the circumstances within which we must live. However, your essential self never goes away.

It is always available for rediscovery, and in fact rediscovery of this part of you is essential to your reinvention. Your essential self goes beyond the skills that you have learned throughout your life. It is the place of knowing who you are, what you are most passionate about, and how you want to live.

As you look for your own essential self, you will see examples of other people who have successfully found their essential selves—like the corporate executive turned author, the artist who has spent most of her life serving her family, or the technical engineer who became a travel writer. The *Huffington Post* did an article on men and women over fifty who had reconnected with their essential selves and was pleasantly surprised by the extraordinary stories that came in. One such story was of Lisa from Salt Lake City, who at fifty-six and single went to Italy on her own. She discovered she was strong, wise, and courageous and knew in that moment she wanted to live in Italy. She returned to Florence to live full-time.

Sensory self amnesia, which is forgetting the essential truth of who you are, is not something to be sad about; it is something to acknowledge and become aware of in your day-to-day life. Awareness of your physical, emotional, and thinking selves is an important step in the reinvention equation. Without awareness, you do not have the information you need to make the changes that are called for in your life now.

When our lives are turned on their ears, we get antsy about setting them straight as soon as possible because our egos, speaking from our adapted selves, instruct us to get back to where we were. We are addicted to certainty. We believe that if we can put things in order, we will have less stress and more balance. This delusional idea of the necessity of certainty is borne out of our experiences as children and carried into adulthood unexamined.

Once we realize and accept we have sensory self amnesia, then we can continue our hero's journey with much more sense of being in uncertainty, which is not such a bad thing.

The Truth of Our Being

We lost touch with the truth of our being a long time ago. The process started as soon as we were born because we had to adapt to live in our families. Adaptation is not wrong. It is just the way we humans develop from babies to adults. We forget who we are because our adapted behaviors become unconscious. Then when trauma occurs, we are thrown into disruption, sometimes beyond what we think we are capable of handling. This is both the challenge and the opportunity.

As we turn inward to examine our authentic natures and challenge our habitual patterns, we uncover the rich treasures of our souls and the meaning of our lives. For so many years we have operated as though our adapted patterns are who we are when they are just the way we have been acting. Like actors, on the stage of life we have learned and played the parts requested of and taught to us in order to be accepted and loved and acknowledged for our achievements. Now our world has blown into pieces. We are called to live from a new place.

A Changing World

Many of us tend to go into negative states after trauma, blaming ourselves for what has happened. However, that is not helpful to our journey, nor will it help us to move forward with the courage and presence that are called for at this stage.

We feel a lack of confidence because we are angry and sad about the way things have turned out. We expected more or better things in our lives at this age. We have worked hard in all areas of our lives and are confused about how things seem to have gone so far off the rails. In reality nothing has gone off the rails. We live in a fast-changing world in which once-successful companies have now disappeared. Take Kodak, for example. Who would have guessed that a company that controlled large portions of the photographic paper market in 1998 would be bankrupt and out of business a few years later? Now all our photos are taken using digital cameras, which most of us have in our cell phones.

Imagine what jobs will no longer be needed in the future. At the same time what new careers might be spawned by technological phenomena? The innovations taking place in our society now are in no way creating certainty. We are living in a world of constant flux with the old going out fast and the new coming into being with a shorter life span than ever before. There is an urgent need to look inside ourselves and once again reestablish our connection to our souls. You might call this essential self the truth of who you are. It is the purity of being present when a baby first arrives in this world. We all have it. Most of us have forgotten about it in the face of years of training and habitual adaptation that have left us with seemingly few options as we confront the upheavals in our lives.

As you progress on the hero's journey, you must open to knowing once again the truth of your being. Doing this is a stripping away of the adaptations and standing naked in front of the mirror of your life with all the bulges and sags and hair growing where it didn't use to and still saying, "I love you."

We also sometimes go into a state in which our ego voice says, "I'm right." This kind of thinking will keep us stuck for a long time if we choose to stay there. It won't help us move to the next step in the process. It will also block the voices of our hearts and the voices of greater energy.

Faith

When tough things happen, our faith is shaken. We need to know who we are and what we stand for. Marylin, who turned fifty this year, was in a funk because she had recently broken up with her boyfriend and had never been married. She took some time to examine her life and decided to embrace her singleness. Marriage was off the table, so she went about her life doing the things she loved and embracing her community of friends who loved and supported her. She let go of the idea of marriage and was calm, confident, and centered in her own life. This accomplishment came from her work on her journey to find the truth of her being. When we connect with our essential selves, our choices become clear, our awareness is at an all-time high, and we are courageous in our daily activities as we take on the tough tasks that show up. Reinvention is a process of discovery by looking at our values, skills, and attitudes to remind ourselves of how good we really are. There are many great aspects to ourselves we may take for granted, and now is the time to affirm them.

When I broke my ribs riding my bike, I treated the injury like no big deal. I just kept on going in the same way, feeling pain every time I took a breath. The experience was not serious enough to me to bring me to a full stop and make me ask what was going on.

The serious break of my ankle was a bit more of a challenge to pass off as no big deal, as it had a greater impact on my day-to-day life. My attitude was to deal with it as a medical issue rather than a life issue. Therefore I undertook the healing process and physiotherapy with due diligence like the good planner and worker I was. Nothing really had to change. I just had to work hard at getting the ankle back into working order.

Then came the cancer experience. Cancer has a way of stopping you in your tracks because of the life-threatening aspects of the disease. My life was on the line. At least that was how I felt about it. That feeling generated a deep sadness in me. I cried tears of regret as to how I had lived my life up until then. Then the basic question of, Do I want to live? rose to the surface. When you are faced with that question, you must make a choice. My choice was to live. I then asked myself, How will I live?

When Life Is Good

Trauma can trigger various responses from us depending on our histories, our adapted ways of living, and our beliefs about ourselves. Just imagine for a moment that we did not have to experience trauma to realize we want to live our lives differently. What if we just recognized the time is here and now to make the journey of reinvention? Life is not static. We live in a dynamic, fluid world changing in local and global ways that will affect our lives in some way. Even if you believe your life is just fine, now is the time to wake up and be aware of what is going on around you so you can participate in your reinvention from inspiration rather than desperation.

In looking back I can affirm my patience, loyalty, and persistence. I learned to be a planner, so I constantly try to head off any wrong turn. I have learned, though, that I can't control everything or plan for every event. At the same time changes to the plan are always hard for me. Don't ask me to change direction in the moment. My planning process takes precedence, so I will fight to stay on the track I am on even if there is good evidence that a change would be better. My awareness of the need to change direction helps in the adjustment, but still it can be a fearful moment. Awareness is especially helpful in the process of reinvention because we need to be present to change with new information being provided.

I now also know from my personal review that I love to teach. My love for teaching has been a theme of my life, so this information is important to pay attention to and not bypass. The question becomes then, how can I apply what I know I love and am good at?

All of us have transferable skills that can be used to switch from one path to another. Our job is to figure out what those skills and attitudes are so that we can see how they might match to the new path we are taking. One such example is a technical manger I coached who was a genius at getting people to work together and collaborate, a real people person. When he was fired from his technical career, he reinvented himself as a call center manager for a major food chain. He brought his people-management skills to a company that needed those skills.

Faith in yourself is a key element in reinvention. Remember who you are no matter the circumstances around the ending that has brought you to this new path.

Questions to Consider

1. How do I want to live my life?
2. What do I know about the truth of who I am?
3. Do I have the courage to get past my ego?

Chapter 7

Paying Attention

Paying attention to the things that you value in life is fundamental to your happiness.

—Elisha Goldstein

As I write this morning, I am on the southwest coast of Ireland watching the wild waves of the Atlantic Ocean crash against the shore. The rain has been pounding and the wind blowing most of the night. Now there is the most magnificent rainbow, the lower tip of it landing in the field right in front of my door. As I ran outdoors early to try to get a picture, I was lashed with rain, and the cold wind blew back what hair I have left on my head, giving me a chill. It was the most exhilarating full-body feeling. We not only need these experiences but must live in them to get the full sense of being in our lives.

Much has been written about living in the present moment. Teachers tell us we are better able to live our lives when we are aware and live in the circumstances appearing right now. Why? Simply because what is occurring now is where the action is. The past is already gone and cannot be changed. Whatever happened is behind you, so there is no benefit to rolling around in the rubble of the past.

It will only make you sad or angry or both and leave you with little energy to deal with what is here now.

The future is not here yet. However, many of us have been taught to plan for a number of future scenarios to avoid catastrophe. As one of my management friends said to me, we plan for the future to avoid the iceberg we know is coming but can't see yet.

Planning for the future has its benefits but little relevance to the present moment. Much planning has been done on false data that everyone thought was true. The longer the state of affairs looks stable, the more we are certain things will stay the same for a long time. We forget how fast times can change and how little control we have over many matters.

Still, because of the outward focus of Western thinking, we grasp for certainty whenever we can. This illusion keeps us from being in the moment.

When going through reinvention, it is imperative to live in the moment. The future is unknown, so there is no point worrying about future outcomes that may never come to pass.

Present-Moment Living

It is time to work from the inside out. This contradicts most of our training and adaptation as children. It is also the time for us to be awake to what is being shown to us. It is time to listen to the impulse, as Barbara Marx Hubbard, a futurist and author, would say. Her biography is an inspiring story of how we can learn to live in the present moment. She is the president and cofounder of the Foundation for Conscious Evolution. Born in 1929, Barbara was a mother of five children and became depressed as she struggled to find meaning in her life. When the bombs were dropped on Japan, she started to ask, "What is the meaning of our new power that is for good?" Barbara was sixteen years old at the time. Her search for the answer to this question has guided her life. This is the search for meaning all of us can take for our own lives. When we know what matters to us in the moment, then we know the path will be there as we take the steps.

Barbara Marx Hubbard is the perfect example of what this book is all about. As her autobiography states, her journey started with her reading *Toward a Psychology of Being* by Abraham Maslow, who said that every self-actualizing person has one thing in common: a chosen vocation they find intrinsically self-rewarding.

Barbara has lived moment to moment in search of conscious evolution. She believes that we are all on a path of evolution. Some of us just don't know it. One lesson of present-moment living that we can take from Barbara's work is study. She studied the great masters who wrote about consciousness and transition, such as Sri Aurobindo, the great Indian sage, who said, "Man is a transitional species."

Present-moment living is a challenge for many of us because there are so many distractions that get in the way all day long. However, there are certain skills we can learn to help us live in the moment. Present-moment living is a constant practice because we are continually distracted by outside influences.

Meditation is one tool. You can start slowly. There is no need to try to be perfect at it when you start. I often ask people just to take ten minutes to sit and breathe. Instantly you will notice how your mind wanders from one topic to the next. That's okay and natural.

Over time the mind becomes more quiet. It is difficult to understand there is nowhere to get to. Again our outward focus has us setting goals and challenges to be at a certain point at a certain time. This is not necessary in meditation.

Just start, even if you tell yourself you don't have time. Be diligent with yourself and give yourself the gift of a few minutes of quiet breathing. This is not a quick fix for anything, but it has been proven to help people be more present in the moment, think more clearly, and feel more calm in the face of adversity. Meditation is a building block of the reinvention process. It is scientifically proven to help.

Exercise is another present-moment activity that brings you into your physical body. Personally, I use a daily yoga practice to engage not only my body but also my attentive mind. I find yoga to be calming and centering.

The third skill you can learn is awareness. This might seem simple, but with distractions all around, to be aware of your body, feelings, and thinking at all times is a challenging task. However, with practice it is possible to tune in to your whole self to see how you are in the moment.

Questions to Consider

1. How often do I pay attention?
2. When was the last time I felt really alive?
3. Can I meditate a few minutes every day?

Chapter 8

Listen to the Impulse

I actually think every person can make a difference. Every single human being has within the impulse to express more of who they truly are.

—Barbara Marx Hubbard

We humans by nature are designed to evolve and have evolved from the humblest of beginnings. Whether you acknowledge it or not, you are constantly changing and evolving. Listening to the impulse is listening to your intuitive voice as it encourages you to follow a particular path.

It can be scary to go into the shadow of the unknown. Don't give up. It is by going though the valley of shadow within us that we open to the light and a new way of thinking about ourselves.

There are four parts of us involved in the transformative process: the intellect, the heart, the intuition, and the body. Each of these plays a part as we reinvent ourselves.

While on vacation in Ireland, I met Claire, who is in her late seventies and lives on the outskirts of a small village on the Atlantic Coast of Ireland. How on earth did I find her? I listened to what other people said and knew I had to meet her. I am fascinated by people who live life to the fullest every day. Claire is such a person. She is a wonderful example for those of us seeking to reinvent our lives. She has done so many times in her life. She has been a wife, mother, and traveler, and now she is an intuitive reader of life for those who are open to what she has to say. All her life she has lived in Ireland and traveled the world. She lives in a small two-bedroom home on a high prominence of rock overlooking the Atlantic Ocean. Her garden is protected from the wind by windswept trees and low, thick, entangled green bushes with bright-yellow flowers. Hundreds of seashells, which people have brought to her from all over the world, are scattered about the garden, mixed among a collection of odd garden gnomes that seem to stare at you. As I stood looking out over the land and the steep drop to the ocean, the wind whipped my face, and I felt alive. She called me in for my meeting with her. She is an oracle, a reader of life, and a listener.

Her recent trip to India with an old friend raised more than a few eyebrows. People thought her silly to take such a long, arduous journey, especially at her age. People ask her, "Why do you do these things?" She says because she can. Why not? she asks. She believes in what life brings her. She listens to the impulse within her to guide her in her life. She says there is no need to hurry; just pay attention to the energy.

This is the impulse in action. I was thrilled to meet her on the very day I started this chapter on following the impulse. She is the best example of what I am talking about.

Being Open to Impulse

You have the same opening to impulse that Claire does. It is within all of our capacities to hear and feel the impulse; whether you activate it or not is up to you.

Some might call being open to impulse *following your heart* or *listening to your intuition*. In whatever way you know it for yourself, make it a critical part of your reinvention journey.

Intuitive forces are at work to push us all to take the hero's journey. If you fail to make the journey, you do so at great cost to yourself and those around you. While those around you have no control over your journey, they are tied to it as they are to their own.

Your inner wisdom is calling now. Listen to the impulse to take the journey of your life. It will be one journey of many perhaps, and at this time it is the necessary one. Do not turn back. Have the courage to follow what is shown to you.

What would you see and hear if you were able to step aside from yourself and be the observer? You would hear the strong voice of your ego trying to persuade you to go back. Why? Simply because the nature of the old part of you is to keep things the way they were. The old way was a place of comfort and certainty. To take a new road creates fear, and that triggers the ego response to keep things the same.

Yet your heart knows the truth. It also has a voice, though its voice is gentle and shy and soft. There is a part of you that knows the old way is unsustainable. In some way you have a desire to change your life, and now is the time to do it.

Listen to your heart, and let the impulse carry you on the path of the next iteration of your life.

This is not a simple journey. Even with the fear and doubt, go forward with your heart open and aware of what life is bringing. Feel your pulse race as you take the next step, and know you will be supported on your hero's journey.

Questions to Consider

1. How am I like Claire?
2. What is the impulse of my life saying to me?
3. Am I willing to make the investment to learn my heart's voice?

Chapter 9

Love

This is the most challenging activity that humans get into, which is love. You know, we have the sense that we cannot live without love, that life has very little meaning without it.

—Leonard Cohen

The Atlantic Coast of Ireland is called "the Wild Atlantic Way." I am sure it has this name because of the wild weather, the rugged coastline, and the extraordinary beauty. There is something about the weather here that brings you back to your roots. It is wild, wet, cold, and driven by the wind. I have stepped outside in a storm and almost gotten blown back into the house from the nor'wester wind carrying rain and cold. You can smell the wet earth and the salty sea air. The area fills every part of my being with aliveness, love, and a feeling of being grounded like nowhere else I have ever been. It is a feeling of being totally alive and in love. I have learned that within us we all have a love for ourselves and the amazing planet we live on. This love rises up when we see, feel, and fill ourselves up with the beauty that always surrounds us, no matter where we happen to be.

This love is the impulse of life, and it guides us. The impulse talks to us like a rabbit peeking out from behind a tree, asking us to pay attention. This is such an important part of the reinvention journey. The gentle call from within our essential selves is critical to listen for. When we hear it, we can know we are being guided to our next step. For example, I had my dog at a certain day care for a long time, but over a few weeks I began feeling uneasy about leaving him there. One morning I woke up and could feel in my body it was time to take him out of that day care. There was nothing wrong on the surface. I was being informed intuitively, through my essential self, as to what action to take. I believe listening to these impulses is an important element of awakening to and following the guidance of our essential selves.

We don't need to run off to the most rural places to hear the call from within. With practice we can teach ourselves to hear the still, small voice when we are in our own homes. When you are faced with busy days, noisy children, and bosses' demands, train yourself to stop for a moment and hear the voice of the impulse. It will always guide you.

The hero's journey is a challenging one yet can be seen as an evolutionary step in personal transformation that will lead to a new way to see and be in your life.

Most of us were trained from a young age to work hard, be loyal, and stay with one company or partner as long as possible, preferably a lifetime. I have met more than one couple who wake up after the kids are gone not knowing who they or their partner are. So much time has gone by in which they've forgotten to create a rich, vibrant relationship by letting the focus of attention be the work to be done, their careers, and the raising of their children. This is a time for the reinvention journey. Most people do not know where to start because the void seems so big. Imagine the gut-wrenching tightness when you look at your partner and ask yourself, *Who is this person?* It is a scary moment. It is a moment of choice—a moment of choice to reinvent yourself; the relationship, if possible; and, in doing so, your life.

Alcohol was my fuel for getting ahead in the world. It was a way of keeping the emotions not expressed for many years in their closet. It allowed me to pretend to be someone I wasn't. A quiet, introspective man, I became outgoing and talkative, trying to be the life of the party. It was an adapted way of getting through my life that I thought was effective. But I was listening to my ego voice tell me that there was no problem, that everything was fine. The morning after a night of drinking was a time of rationalization and self-talk to assure myself my life was working well. Over time the neural connections in our brains set up in patterns that keep us stuck in places we don't see are harmful. That is why when I walked late into the conference hall of fifty of my colleagues from around the world and there was only one vacant seat, my ego could still say, "See how important you are? They saved your seat for you." This was my denial of a problem I did not think I had. The reality was I was late because of my hangover from the night before.

In order to reinvent our lives we need a more clear and powerful reason than the one keeping us stuck. My boss spoke to me about being late for the meeting knowing full well what was going on. I know now he was attempting to bring my attention to my drinking problem without coming right out and saying it. My denial kept me in the dark until sometime later in the year when I was fired, and then the reason for reinvention became clear and powerful. Your reason for reinvention may not come to you in a loud or jolting way. It may be a gentle suggestion, or you may hit a wall and know it is time. In any case the reason to take the hero's journey will be made clear, and then you are free to choose.

Self-Love

We often forget we have the power of choice in all aspects of our lives. One of my choices was shifting from using alcohol to power my way through anything in front of me to using self-love. How we adapt to and take on our adult circumstances has a lot to do with the training we got as children. The more we push and try hard and grunt at our circumstances, the less we can hear the still, small voice of the impulse.

We take action on that which is before us. Do it in a more mindful and attentive manner. The reinvention journey is one in which you accept who you are, the value you bring, and the possibilities that will be revealed.

You do not have to worry about what the results are in the moment. There is an element of getting going that has you know you have done your best for right now, and that is all that is called for.

Letting go and allowing are two of the aspects of the journey. You do your work, whatever that is for the day, and then you allow it to percolate like coffee, becoming robust with flavor as it bubbles in the pot. I was brought up to be competitive, to push hard for the goal, and to work harder if times got tough. The reinvention journey involves allowing rather than pushing. It is about listening to your essential self rather than plowing ahead no matter what.

Self-love is also an attribute of the reinvention journey. Remember to love yourself enough to allow whatever shows up to be the right thing in the moment. It does not matter what it is. Each turn in the road and every person who shows up is a signpost on the journey. Bring your awareness to these guiding lights during the day.

My wife and I were in London recently and decided to go uptown one evening. Now, London is a huge city, and getting around is a challenge. It took us forty-five minutes to get to our destination. The night was cold and windy, typical for March, but we were not dressed for the weather.

After dinner, we called the taxi company recommended by our hotel, and the dispatch told us it would take them twenty minutes to get to us. The traffic in London is such a twisted mass of vehicles that I knew in my gut that there was no way that the taxi would show up that quickly. Instead of paying attention to what my intuition was telling me, I listened to the inaccurate information from the dispatch.

We waited for almost an hour before canceling the taxi and

hailing one from the street. I realized later that the dispatcher was only trying to be helpful by giving us a short pickup time. At the same time I was in my adapted self and so tried to honor my agreement to wait for the taxi I had called without regard for the chilling cold my wife and I felt standing out in the wind.

What does this have to do with love? Well, I needed to love myself as I reflected on what had happened. I immediately felt that I had let down the driver whom we had called. Now he would be waiting for us, and we would not be showing up. Sometimes things do not go as planned. We need to be gentle enough with ourselves to allow for whatever has happened and carry on. No one was hurt, with the exception of us being cold and the driver waiting for us. The unavoidable will always occur when you least expect it. Let it go. Send love and good wishes to yourself and take a breath. There is nothing to push against to make it right because what is in the past is in the past. It cannot be changed, but your reaction to it can.

Questions to Consider

1. How do I show myself love?
2. Do I notice when I am using my adaptive strategies?
3. What old self-blame do I hold on to that I can let go of?

Chapter 10

The Hero Has Roots

If we shift our center of attention to gratitude we will have, for the first time, sufficiency.

—Julio Olalla

In all that I've learned through my journey of reinvention, I've come to the conclusion that we are all more similar than we realize. For example, I would guess that, just like me, you have a deep, ongoing pull to return to your roots, that place from whence you came before you knew yourself as you do today. It is a simple place where there are no complications and a clarity of soul that you remember from long ago, perhaps in a different time. When you imagine the feeling of this place, your physical self relaxes, and there is an ease not present in the everyday fast pace of the here and now.

Rootedness

Our forefathers were rooted in the land, and they arguably had a harder life than we do. It is difficult to know what they felt and thought. Still it seems they had a clarity of pursuit and a simpler life. You can feel this sense of rootedness on the wild west coast of

Ireland, where I am writing right now. The area is primarily rocky, so there is little cultivation. The farmers carve out a living with milk cows, sheep, and vegetable gardening.

The farms and homes have been passed down from generation to generation, at least up until now. The sadness is prevalent as the young people leave to find work in the city. The older folk wonder if the young generation can sustain their rootedness in the cities. This melancholy philosophizing won't change anything necessarily, but there is an awareness of history the elders want to pass on.

We must be prepared when we choose to take the hero's journey and reinvent our lives. The challenges we will face, the fear that will roll through our bodies, and the conditions under which we will live take physical, emotional, and intellectual energy. We must be prepared for the journey even when it comes at the most unexpected times. To be prepared means to recognize that we live in an ever-changing world and so need to pay attention to what is going on. Awareness is the first key to recognizing you are on the journey, and preparation calls for you to know where you are in your journey. That means taking the time to stop and take inventory of your life. What is working, and what is not? What is done and needs to be put aside?

History Teaches

I realized something on the wet March day that my wife and I traveled up the Irish coast to Kenmare. We'd hired a colorful local driver. He was seventy years old, and he'd started a bus and taxi company after quitting farming a few years prior.

He showed us his land, where he lived in what had once been his parents' home. "I was born in that house," he said. "See that window on the second story? That was my bedroom." He showed us his brothers' houses and his daughter's house close to his in the town of Castletownbere. His stories were wrapped in the history of the fisheries, sheep raising, and farming in the community. There was a sense that the people here looked out for one another, helped each other, and were respectful of one another.

The sheep also were raised together in a community, all grazing on the same land. In order to tell them apart each farmer painted them a different color.

I said, "It must be a lot of work for the farmers to get the sheep off the mountain."

"The dogs do that," he replied.

Being from the city, I asked what I am sure he thought was a stupid question. "How do the dogs know what color they are looking for?"

"No, no, no," he responded indignantly. "The dogs get all the sheep and bring them to the corral."

Does the hero need a community? I think so.

That was what our driver was really saying when he showed us all his relatives' houses. He was showing us his rooted, long-lasting community that had been around for hundreds of years.

Our driver had lost his wife to cancer nine years ago. They'd been married for thirty-four years. He'd made it through his hero's journey with the help of his community. He knows how to take care of himself, yet the community helped and still does when his family gets together for special occasions. The whole community participates in the births, baptisms, confirmations, and birthdays among the different families. Their roots are deep. We can learn from them how to better navigate the reinvention journey.

Our driver took us through the Healy Pass, a magnificent hand-built road high in the hills connecting one village to another. It was built in 1840 as a government project to keep the people from starving. There is a beauty, a ruggedness, and a rootedness you feel when you stand on the highest point surrounded by sheep and long grass. You cannot help but feel the souls of the men who built this road. Their souls were part of the reinvention of the time, doing what was necessary to stay alive.

As I stood there, I thought about the disconnect we fast-paced city folk have with the land and our souls. We are floating around trying to find a place to call home. At this age and stage, disgruntled by our circumstances and recognizing reinvention is at hand, it is more important than ever to have awareness of where we are and who we are awakened to on the journey.

Do you know how to find your rootedness? You may have roots in your extended family and engage them as your touchstone. If you are like me, family is not where your roots are. I ground myself in my daily life right where I am. I take solace and comfort from the amazing woman I am married to and the close friends I have. Being present is being awake to finding your rootedness. When you are present, you are aware how you feel. When your mind is attentive, it is more flexible, and you are more receptive to your internal and external environment.

Mindfulness in Action

Being present is mindfulness in action. Through the learned practice of mindfulness we become more aware, and the more aware we are, the more present we are to the moment. This shows in our energy with whomever we are with.

Often when we take the hero's journey of reinvention, we are not consciously aware of our roots. These are the places we call home. They are places we know and can take comfort from. They give us confidence that we belong someplace. As we are called to take the journey, it can feel as if we are tearing ourselves away from those places of comfort. When this happens, it is most important to bring ourselves back to the present moment because this is where we will find the strength and courage to continue on the journey.

The essence of the hero's journey at this point is to be fully present as best we can with the conscious awareness that we are out of our places of comfort and familiarity.

We can also find temporary resting places or ways to nourish ourselves as we reinvent ourselves. This is where practices such as yoga, meditation, or walking the dog can be helpful. Using such tools will signal our brains that we have landed, if only for a few minutes. Then we can take a few minutes to tap into the voice of impulse, which is more available to us when we are present in the moment. I see people work hard. They have discomfort and face challenges, yet their present-moment awareness allows them to face what has to be faced with courage and tenacity and strength.

Opening Channels of Higher Awareness

As I walked along the rural road today, the sheep were in the fields next to me. I could smell the sweet, pungent odor of their manure. It was beautiful. The serenity in my heart pulsed through my body like a soft wind.

The sea was crashing onto the beach a ways to my right. I could smell the surf and taste the salt and feel the wetness on my jacket. The chill went through my bones, and I smiled. Inside myself I felt at home, rooted in this strange land I had only come to visit a few days ago.

This is the secret I learned today. If you are in a reinvention process, you must find ways to root yourself to the earth every day. It opens your channels to higher levels of awareness within you. Stay aware and connected to your roots.

We need to recreate experiences like this for ourselves no matter where we are and what is going on. In the busiest and scariest of moments when we are not sure we can continue on our hero's journey, we can stop for a moment and breathe. Our breath is the anchor to our presence. Then we can take a walk in silence even if it is for just a few minutes. This in itself is a practice that will support our hero's journey.

The road can be hard and the challenges almost beyond what we believe we can handle. Yet within us burns the flame of courage and determination.

Questions to Consider

1. What am I grateful for today?
2. Am I feeling rooted now?
3. Do I feel the breath of life within?

Chapter 11

You Can Do It!

You are not stuck where you are, unless you decide to be.
                                                                —Wayne Dyer

It wasn't supposed to be this way, but this is the way it is. We were given an optimistic picture from our parents of a life that included education, hard work, a marriage with kids, one employer for life, and retirement at fifty-five with the joy of travel and ease on the horizon. We all bought into this scenario, and for some time it looked like our lives would go according to plan. Then the world changed before our eyes faster than we could have imagined.

So now reinventing ourselves has become a necessity at an age and stage when we did not expect to have to work this hard to maintain what we have much less retire. A friend of mine says now he is on the retire-at-ninety plan.

In order to bring robustness, shape, and substance to our reinvention equation, we need tools and skills to help us along the way. I have already outlined some of these, but review is always good to remind us of what we need along the way.

Make the Choice

The first skill is the ability to make conscious decisions. You must make a conscious and specific choice to reinvent your life even though the path is not completely clear. In the face of fear and doubt you still have to make the choice and dedicate yourself to remaking it over and over again if you have to. You may have to leave relationships or careers behind as you move forward on your new path. These are not easy choices to make, but they are necessary to learn more deeply what you need.

Neuroscientists say that when you make a conscious choice, you signal your brain to organize the electrical impulses to support the choice. This gives you momentum. When you start, it is like moving a train; it takes a lot of energy, but then it gets easier as momentum carries you along.

Always remember you have the power to choose, but also know that you will be held accountable for your choices. You should use this power of choice with a consciousness of what your desired outcome is. We make our best choices when we combine the tools and skills described in this book. There is little to be gained by choosing from negativity, revenge, anger, or sadness.

The ego self is active and alive as a part of us. Be aware of your ego and how it influences your decisions. It will always be with you, but it is better to have it help you and others in a positive way rather than a negative one.

You can approach the change in your life using old habits and old ways and old thinking, using learned behaviors and conditioned responses, or you can apply mindfulness to the situation and expand the range of possibilities. When you choose mindfulness, you feel a sense of openness and acceptance of not only what is but also what can be. Even though you can't see the whole picture and don't know how your new life will show up, your inner attitude is calm and yet persistent.

Awareness

The second skill is awareness. This skill takes practice because many of us are used to going about our lives without paying attention to what and who is around us or checking in to see how we feel in the moment. It seems simple on the surface, but I have found maintaining awareness a challenging skill that takes practice to master.

I have a dog who loves to chase rabbits. He has taught me awareness because if he sees the rabbit first, the chances are I will be on the end of the leash trying to run with a seventy-pound dog that has only one goal: to catch the rabbit. His awareness of me has gone to zero, and my awareness of him and the rabbit has escalated to 100 percent. So when we go for a walk, I am on high alert for rabbits. It is wonderful practice because I take this awareness into other areas of my life.

As an example, I practice yoga five days a week. I have found a new level of awareness of my body and mind that has deeply enriched my practice. I have my dog to thank for that.

Meditation

Meditation is a useful tool along the hero's journey. There are various forms of meditation, and you could study them for a long time. My preference is the simple approach. Sit down, close your eyes, and focus on your breathing. Then become aware of your self-talk without judgment. You choose the amount of time you wish to meditate on a daily basis. My personal choice is twenty minutes twice a day. Meditation is a tool I use to bring me back from all the business of the world and to let the energy flow through me as it will. It almost seems counterintuitive to be doing something that has no objective except to sit and breathe, but I have found it to be a well of wisdom and insight made available with a gentleness I appreciate. I have developed a sharper awareness of my day-to-day life from regular meditation. I tend to pay attention to when stress shows up in my body, look for what is causing the stress, and see if there is a way to reduce it. The time between noticing what is going on in my life and taking some form of action has been reduced significantly through the use of mediation.

Self-Compassion

Self-compassion also plays a huge role in the reinvention journey. Take the time to speak to yourself in a compassionate way, and bring gratitude forward for your life at every opportunity. It has been proven that speaking gratitude for your life changes everything. It is not a quick fix, but it will sustain you for the challenging journey of reinvention. Every day make a list of at least five things you are grateful for. Then repeat them to yourself during the day.

Throughout your day you need to take time to bring self-compassion to yourself. In a busy day, I recommend at least a two-minute break every hour to remind yourself of self-love and self-care.

There is too much stress and negativity in life today, especially when we are reinventing our lives as we know them. An antidote is needed to keep us healthy and at more optimal operating levels.

So walk more slowly, consider the circumstances, and make choices with awareness.

Journaling

Another tool is journaling. It has been found when you pick up a pen and paper and start to write that you connect the hand to your heart and brain. The technique of free writing wherein you just start to write may reveal elements of your personal self that will be of help on this path.

Wayne Dyer once said he had journals going back many years. When you write every day as he did, after a time, you have your autobiography on your shelf, a story of your life with all your insights, mistakes, and successes that will live forever and be told again and again. Journaling is helpful to create a history of your life and also useful to work through whatever is going on in your life. David Allen, author of *Getting Things Done*, says writing things down clears the clutter from your mind. Other research shows writing is an excellent tool for letting you see what you know and may make you more productive since it clears the mind.

In *The Buddha's Brain*, Dr. Rick Hansen describes the negative bias of our brains. One negative experience outweighs one hundred positive ones. Our brains have a Velcro-like quality when it comes to negative experiences, but positive ones flash by unless we specifically hold on to the emotional feeling of them for some time, for twenty to thirty seconds. This technique allows for the positive experience to be stored. In this way we can, as Hansen points out, "take in the good."

We can practice this technique, and as we do so, we can change the way our neurons connect and therefore change our future experiences. Dr. Hanson says that when we highlight our milestones and our successes and hold on to them for even a brief period of time, it moves the experience from short-term memory to long-term memory, which changes the neural patterns in our brains. We need this change to reinvent the experiences of our lives. This is good news, as it means it is possible to change our thinking selves.

Pandiculation

When dogs and cats stretch after getting off the couch, their whole bodies are involved in a gentle motion of moving from the tip of the nose to the end of the tail, and then they completely relax. This is pandiculation.

Martha Peterson describes pandiculation as "a conscious, voluntary contraction of a muscle—tighter than it already is—followed by a slow, deliberate and active lengthening of that muscle, followed by a complete relaxation." Pandiculation allows the brain to reset its communication with the muscles so that they can move more freely.

When I interviewed Martha, author of *Move without Pain* and one of the world's foremost teachers of body movement, we discussed at length the connection between the brain and the muscular and nervous systems of the body. Somatics, of which Martha is an expert, is learning to reduce and eliminate pain by teaching the brain and muscles how to communicate effectively after they have been stuck in a loop that keeps the muscles tight.

Pandiculation is one such technique that helps the brain and muscles to interact properly again, and it is one of the most important tools we can use in the reinvention journey. Whereas Martha's teaching is specifically about the brain-muscle connection, we have been speaking here about the brain-emotion connection.

When you have sensory emotional amnesia, the brain and the feelings center are in a loop that prevents the expression of certain feelings. If you never express anger and in fact have suppressed the emotion of anger, then the feedback loop to the brain is stuck. Pandiculation is the conscious choice to express the emotions put away a long time ago and to be aware of how you feel in the moment. Once you've expressed the emotions, relax fully into your awareness and examine how you sense your physical and emotional bodies. The secret is to intentionally bring awareness to what you are doing and how you are feeling. With practice, this process will change your neural patterns over time.

Pandiculation is stretching in an emotional way you haven't for a long time. Like a kid exploring something new, you do it with curiosity and without judgment. You just notice the feeling rising in you and wonder, *What does this mean?* You are the doer and the observer, looking and examining the feeling self as if you haven't met before, though you know it has always been there under the surface. You consciously let it rise up with childlike innocence.

Pandiculate your emotions to enhance your experience. Learning to process your emotions is one of the most important skills you can develop in reinventing your life. When you learn to express your emotions, you in turn learn to process them so that they don't stay stuck in your body. Part of this skill is first being aware that the emotion is present. You may notice a heaviness if you are sad. Then you can identify the emotion, saying, "I feel sad." You may feel a surge of energy if you are angry or a feeling of lightness if you are joyful.

When you have the opportunity, you will want to talk with someone you trust about your experience of going from not expressing emotions to being aware of them and accepting them. The act of speaking about your process is a powerful way of locking in the experience. You can ask yourself the following questions to help bring clarity: What brought on the feeling? How did it feel in your body? What did you notice about your self-talk at the time of the feeling? The energy created by an emotion is like a river. It needs a place to flow. When you consciously engage with an emotion, then its power is taken away, and you can release it over time in a conscious, self-compassionate way. I remember when I started letting myself feel anger. It was outrage at injustice. At first it was like being with a stranger, and then it blossomed into an understanding that anger is one of the feelings I can express from time to time in a healthy way. When I was angry, I would go to the gym and run on the treadmill longer and harder than I usually would. This released the energy and brought me to a more calm feeling, one in which I was pleased to have acknowledged the anger. Now when the anger comes, it comes with awareness and acceptance, and I know I can do something with it. My emotional pandiculation has led me into new territory. It feels as if I have taken back a part of me that was put away a long time ago. After I express my anger I relax into knowing more deeply who I am with more aspects of myself available than a few minutes ago. Try it for yourself. The reinvention equation is about you as a whole person, accepting and using the great depth and breadth of who you are. It is recognizing and accepting the authentic.

Reinvention is a process of awareness in all aspects of your life. You are heading in a new direction, and the whole path is not clear. That's not a problem, as each day you consciously make choices about your new path. You will notice slippage back into old behaviors, but don't let that discourage you. Just be gentle and make a new commitment to continue.

Presence is an aspect of self-compassion that you need on this journey. Statements of self-compassion such as "May I be grateful," "May I be loving," "May I be understanding," and "May I forgive" will be helpful and supportive of your new life.

The brain does not change in one fell swoop. It does, however, change and reorganize itself when given the proper practice over time.

Reinvention

We do not quit on a whim while taking on a new task. We wake up in the morning excited to see what will be presented while we do our work. We don't sit around waiting for something to happen. There is inner and outer movement.

Reinvention is the same idea. We live in it moment to moment. We take action while also watching for what shows up to excite us and interest us, and we expend our thinking on this journey of discovery. Reinvention is certainly a discovery of who you are and what you are passionate enough about to bring into the world.

Our futures are shaped by not only our responses to what is happening in the moment, which for sure is an important element, but also our inheritance of the past through the neural connections that were made as a result of past experiences.

I started this chapter talking about neuroscience. The study of the brain is an important subject to study so that you understand your power to change your circumstances not withstanding what you might think about your past.

Questions to Consider

1. What choices am I making about my life?
2. Have I taken quiet time today?
3. Am I pandiculating my emotional self?

Chapter 12

Beyond the Hero's Journey

If you follow someone else's way, you are not going to realize your potential.

—Joseph Campbell

You have a craving. The longing to reinvent your life has been growing stronger and stronger by the day. It is a sense that what you have spent the last number of years doing has come to an end. It is, you feel, the time now to make more of a contribution, to accept yourself for who you are, and to not compromise on what you know is true for you. You want the suffering and pain to go away. You have been through so much. The pain is just a dull ache now. You have taken the difficult journey through the trauma to a new understanding of yourself.

This is the transformation that happens when you choose to take the hero's journey.

Longing and Craving

There is no turning back to the old life. There is only going forward.

So what is this longing? It is a desire for more meaning in your life or more authentic expression. You can sense the joy in your longing just beyond your reach while anticipating the fun in its fulfillment. You have made the circle back to what looks like your life. The difference is within you. The external things may look the same, but you are different from the inside out. The awareness you have developed will help you at this time of your life. The urgency to have the next new thing show up, whether it be a job, a relationship, or good health, is something you learn to manage through your moment-to-moment presence. Paying attention to what you feel will allow you to know what to do next.

I had an experience of this when I decided to write this book. My longing to write a book based on the pain I had seen in my clients and friends had been bubbling up in me for a long time. This was the way I chose to do it. You may have something else you want in your life.

You get to say no to things you don't want in your life. You get to choose the way you spend your time, money, and energy. You get to choose the people you hang out with. Through the reinvention journey you clearly see all the possibilities. This comes from awareness of feeling, of paying attention not just to your thinking but also the intuition that is needed right here and right now.

Craving, on the other hand, is an insatiable want for something that can never be satisfied, because it is outside of us. Baby boomers learned to crave the good life. We went into our adult years focused on money, status, and accomplishment. All our goals were external to us, and the harder things got, the harder we worked to make our cravings a reality. Since cravings are external to us, when we are attached to them, we lose touch with the essential self and operate from the adapted self, which is being led by ego.

Patience is called for when our lives are being transformed. It takes time to allow for new things to fit into place.

When we are being put through the wringer, we have a tendency to want to either give up and lie down for a rest or get up and keep moving. I had the deluded notion that if I kept moving, driving for success, without self-awareness, that I would be okay at some point. I did not realize that driving for success without awareness was a process taking place within me. Too bad you are the one who is tripping yourself up now, not someone else or some circumstance. We have to do our internal work every day. When we keep going with our internal workings and external workings in alignment, we achieve results.

I'm not saying it's easy. So many distractions get in the way every day, even every moment, to take us away from what we say we want. My experience, sadly, is seeing people quit just before their next good thing comes along.

You need a persistent focus on your transformation so distractions don't take you off the path.

Being Grounded

You need to be grounded in this journey. We lead busy lives, and we sometimes forget to keep our feet on the ground as we strive for the next best thing. After the hero journey it is time to practice living with your feet on the ground. What does that look like for you?

For me, it was planting herbs in my garden this spring. If you knew me, you would know I used to hate anything to do with gardening. It just seemed like a lot of work to me. Through my expanding awareness I realized I felt like I needed to work in the dirt in the garden at home. This physical work was one of the missing pieces in my life. And so I came up with the idea of planting herbs. An extra payoff was that I had the herbs to use in my salads and cooking all summer.

Another way my life has changed since taking the hero's journey concerns my dog, Toby. He is a wonderful companion. However, he is young so wants to play all the time. I have catered to his needs for many months while complaining to anyone who would listen about how little I get done when he is around. He takes things off my desk, grabs the laundry, and constantly brings toys he wants me to throw for him.

The lesson here is that I can't let external distractions take me away from what I know in my heart needs to be done. For example, when I know it is time to write, various distractions can get in the way, such as answering e-mails, cleaning the house, or making supper. When it is time for reinvention, it is much easier to let myself get distracted than to face the work in front of me. So I have learned to remember the choices I have made about being on the journey and how I want my life to look. If I want to write a book, I must spend time writing, and sometimes I have to put Toby in his kennel.

We are driven in our culture by money and social status. Our egos grasp for importance by looking externally for acknowledgment that we are going to be okay. These drives create an energy within us to scramble around trying to find the next best thing that will take us to where we think we want to go.

However, life after the hero's journey is about living with an authentic connection to who we are. This is what grounding is all about.

Questions to Consider

1. What do I say no to now?
2. Have I put the distractions into their kennel?
3. Do I know my essential self today?

Chapter 13

Living Free

You have everything you need for complete peace and total happiness right now.

—Wayne Dyer

You feel as if you have been through the wringer. You had a career, and you were good at it. Why were you the one chosen to be fired and forced to leave the career you knew and the people you worked with for so long? Were you not dedicated enough? Were you not a team player? So many questions bounce around in your head. This could be your life if you let it be that way.

What is called for is a connection, awareness, and understanding of your internal state of being. When feelings arise, be aware of the rising tide and let the feelings, whatever they are, exist. There is nothing to do about them necessarily in the moment; just observe and feel the energy of the feelings and then the dissipation.

Stay Present in the Moment

The beauty of awareness is that you do not need to react to every little thing that is taking place in the moment; you simply need to stay present in the moment.

Awareness is often talked about as part of mindfulness, which I've spoken about earlier. When you have a mindful presence, you are aware internally and externally as to what is going on.

Knowing how you feel, whether it be joy or sadness or something else, gives you a sense of confidence because when you know how you feel, you are better able to take care of yourself. Feelings that come up do not have to be attached to judgment of whether they are good or bad. They are only something to notice.

Craving for more of everything has been a hallmark of baby boomers. We grew up in an era of significant economic expansion, and abundance was an automatic expectation of our lives. When we crave for something to be other than our experience in the moment, then we are not present to that moment. When trauma occurs and we are jettisoned into the reinvention of our lives, it is a time when we must be present to take the next steps shown to us. Even though the situation may be extremely difficult, there is little point in expending energy wanting things to be different. Instead you should use the skills you have learned to stop and take note of the next step.

The old thinking dissipates slowly. It takes a regular routine to change the neural patterns in our brains. Over time the neurons change connections based on our intentions and choices to have new results. This is exciting because you learn that you don't need to know all the steps. All you have to do is have an intention and then take the steps shown to you as you go along.

The discovery of who you are, with all your bumps and bruises and the turns in the road of your life, is an exciting journey. Although at times it feels like you might die or you want to quit, you don't.

As you persist, the walls and the resistance drop away, and the path is shown to you in a way far easier than you might have imagined.

You have to wait for your path to be revealed. That means quiet time. Meditation is good for the times when you feel as if you have hit the wall. Instead of trying to knock the wall down, sit, close your eyes, and take some quiet time. You will be amazed how this practice helps put things more in order. Your level of anxiety will diminish, and you will be ready to keep going.

Reinvention is not so much something to do as someone to be. It is a renewal and revealing of your values, what you stand for, and what is important to you, and most of all it is an opening to your intuitive self, that heart place, from which flows extraordinary wisdom. All of us have it, and the reinvention process calls it forward.

Here's the important point: all of us have the capacity for reinvention. We just get so comfortable in our cubicles that we forget what's possible. So when your career, your marriage, or your health fails, recognize that you are being called forward to a new version of yourself.

Wasted Time

I am a prostate cancer survivor, and I have lived with the consequences of my radical prostatectomy for more than fourteen years. The prostate is the male center of sexual and reproductive potency. In a radical prostatectomy, all of the prostate and surrounding nerves are removed. The prostate is a complicated and complex part of the body in which nerves and tissue are connected such that it is almost impossible not to injure them in this surgical procedure. After a radical prostatectomy, the male experience of intimacy is never the same. I spent a lot of time being angry at the doctor who performed the surgery, thinking he had done it wrong. How crazy our thinking can be when we are caught up in our egos' need to be right. Now, I can look back and be grateful that for fifteen years I have been cancer-free. I was jettisoned into a reinvention of my life I never expected, and I thank my family and doctor for helping me see that I could still have a fulfilling life.

The time wasted on petty things did not serve me well. In hindsight, I realize that the reinvention equation gave me the confidence to go forward instead of looking backward. If you try to go forward while looking in the rearview mirror, you will probably crash.

Wholeness

The reinvention equation is a process of wholeness. It requires involvement from all parts of you. When we get bumped around, we forget how intelligent we are mentally, emotionally, and spiritually. The spirit in you is strong and smart. Your job in the reinvention process is to reactivate these capabilities within you.

Once you realize that all you need is, in a sense, within you, then you stop looking for what looks like the easier, softer way outside yourself. Now when you engage outside resources, you will know why and how to use them to fulfill your intention.

Attachment

One of the last points to make here is about attachment. Most of us have been taught to achieve, whatever that might look like. I was taught that the harder things got, the harder I was to work, the better show I was to put on, and the less emotion I was to show the world. The message was "Do not let them see how you are feeling, so they can't take advantage of you."

I have since learned the more I crave outside, the harder things are. When you release all attachment to things, then you will have everything you need.

The reinvention process is not just about turning inward and forgetting the real world. I have simply focused on this part of the process because we have all been trained to seek outside goals and treasures. We have worked hard to try to find happiness through achievement and success. We have tried to make others happy in the belief that if they are happy, then we will be happy. However, when you come to a point in your life of reinvention, then you open the door to taking a look at things a bit differently. You begin to live free.

Living Free

As you discover your essential self, you will eventually realize that all your efforts focused on outside goals and treasures, although seeming to bring you things, did not result in internal happiness or satisfaction.

True joy creates a resonance deep inside you. This resonance is an acknowledgment of who you know you are and what you stand for. You then look inward in order to do better work and play in the outside world. The activities you undertake in the world come from the strong foundation of that inner resonance. This creates confidence and awareness.

Living free is a concept derived from the reinvention process. How do we know we are living free? Well, it is a feeling that comes from the inside. I can check in with myself and feel the vibration in my bones, so to speak. Living free takes four steps: intention, choices, practice, and persistence.

Intention

The first step of living free is intention. When you set an intention and make a choice, you set up a framework for yourself from which your activity follows.

For example, let's look at meditation. If you intend to meditate every morning, then make it an irrevocable promise. That is what intention is. You have decided to follow a particular path with awareness, and that path will not change unless evidence is shown to you that a new direction is called for.

We are all adapted from growing up with particular messages about how life works. This is not to say our parents were bad. It is just the way it is. Every parent and other influencer in our young lives taught us how life works. Then we took those messages and made them our own so that by the time we were in our early teens the voices were very familiar.

Choices

Once we are firmly on the reinvention path, we will see the choices we have made in the past and will know the choices available for our future.

My ego voice often says, "Don't bother trying that. You will never make money at it, and money is important." Most of my life I have worked hard to overcome messages like this to prove them wrong. I have made a lot of money, and I have lost a lot of money. I have made some good decisions about money, and I have made some bad decisions.

My work life was based on the premise that if I could only be successful enough, then I could stop these voices from yakking at me on a constant basis. This, of course, was not true.

The voices talking to us constantly initially came from elders, and the power of elders is their authority, which is what caused us to so fully accept their messages in the first place. Have you ever noticed the authority with which a doctor speaks diagnoses? When messages are spoken with authority, we accept them at a deep level without any consideration of whether they are true. Most likely you operate your life with those internal voices as a context.

Practice

The constant yakking of our inner voices is why practicing the skills and techniques provided in this book and being aware are so important to the reinvention process. We don't need to overcome these voices. All we need to do is recognize them when they show up, accept them, and decide if we want to follow them in that moment or choose another direction.

When I undertake a new project, my ego voice is loud and clear because the ego operates from the past. No matter; I get up and go do my work on the project anyway. Now, instead of listening to my ego, I have released the anxiety and the pressure around what the outcome will be.

Instead of having the framework of making a lot of money, I have the framework of bringing value.

I ask myself questions like, How can I bring value to my clients today? What is the next best step I can take right now? How am I feeling in this moment?

Persistence

Living free is recognizing you have been through a process of discovery and now can decide how you want to live. Things rarely unfold quickly, so living free requires patience in the face of one distraction after the other.

However, there is a way through. The training we received in our younger years taught us to go for the goal line. We in North America view the goal as the ultimate way to measure success. If we can get to the goal and show others we have done it, then we can label ourselves as a success, especially when we get the accolades of others. It is what we know.

Freedom in our lives, though, comes from the inside out, not the other way around. Freedom is a feeling in our bones of knowing what the next right thing to do is. It might be to take a time-out and be quiet for an hour rather than rushing away somewhere to check off one more thing from the to-do list.

Living free requires trust and persistence when it looks like nothing is changing or things are moving slowly. Our old belief is that circumstances will change when we push hard to make them go in the direction we demand. We continually grasp for anything that looks like it will take us somewhere. Anywhere seems better than standing still. Our systems, mental, emotional, and physical, are adapted to relate to outside pressures rather than engage with what is happening internally.

Old habits are deeply conditioned into our systems, so we need to keep coming back to our intentions for our lives. The traumas you have faced and gotten through have prepared you for this time of freedom. The action looks different from what you are used to.

Let's look at an example. You're out of a job and are trying to reinvent yourself in some way. Then a big bill that you were not expecting comes in the mail. You were sure you had all your money issues under control. When you open the envelope, your first feeling is probably fear. How the hell did this happen? Your internal critical voice goes into overdrive. It has a lot to say to you about how you made a mess of this situation. How could you let this happen, most especially at a time like this when money is tight? Your inner critic is a big bully, and if you don't take charge, it will take you down the rabbit hole fast. This could take you into a derisive state leaving you incapacitated to make any kind of rational judgment about what to do next.

So the first step is to take a breath and step back. Thank your critic for sharing this, then put it into a separate room and close the door. It's not what you need right now.

Then initiate the freedom technique. There are three steps to make the shift from reacting to the outer experience to feeling whole from the inside.

First, bring your attention to your physical, mental, and emotional states without judgment. Notice what is going on, and say to yourself that it is fine the way it is. This releases the tension.

Check in with your body. How do you feel? Do you feel sensations in certain parts of your body? Where? Don't make any judgments; just notice. Check in with your feelings. What are you feeling in this moment? Anger, fear, and regret may come up. That's okay. Just notice how you feel.

Second, remind yourself of your intention and understanding. Freedom comes with releasing the grasp your critical self has on you and your experiences.

Third, go into a quiet space for a while. Let your inner heart wake up with self-compassion and love reminding you of who you are and what you believe in for your life.

Questions to Consider

1. Do I check in with myself to see how I am feeling?
2. What am I attached to?
3. Do I take the time to be compassionate with myself?

Chapter 14

Embrace the Journey

We must be willing to get rid of the life we've planned, so as to have the life that is waiting for us.

—Joseph Campbell

Many lessons are learned in the time of reinvention. It is like watching the new spring flowers grow. Perhaps in your times of reinvention you have noticed how you are renewed.

The Observer Position

An inner calmness has arisen in my life that did not use to be there. *Worry* was a watchword running my life like a traffic cop directing one internal conversation after another. The worry conversation would come up during the night when my mind was not so busy with day-to-day activities.

One of the skills learned through meditation and mindfulness is how to slow everything down. You may have noticed that with anxiety there is an internal speeding up that happens. When you slow everything down, thinking becomes clearer. You become more adept at taking the observer position rather than being in the fray.

Nonattachment is also a skill you can develop. When situations come up, try not to let your ego get engaged, because that attaches you to an outcome, and then you fall into old habits again. Many people want to be right about life's situations and work hard to prove that point. The reinvention journey will show better results when you give up trying to be right.

Attachment

I love to be right and have for much of my history been attached to the outcome of my rightness. My wife, whom I love dearly, has for most of our marriage been late. I, on the other hand, like to be on time. She does not get upset about being late, because things, she says, will always work out, and that seems to be the case.

In the past, when we were going somewhere, I would be ready well ahead of time, and then I would try to cajole her into getting ready faster by telling her what time it was or letting her know I was going to the car and would meet her there. I learned as a child that it was not polite to let people down, and I took this learning into adulthood. So all the while I would feel tension in my gut due to being attached to the outcome of being on time. Now, I use my awareness to prepare myself for her timing of getting ready, and I let go of the outcome of being on time. It works! I feel much less stress and more curiosity as I wait with patience I did not know I had.

Do we not attach ourselves to outcomes, trying to make things turn out the way we want them to?

Expectations about outcomes leave us worrying, energetically invested in what happens next, and using our energy to try to control aspects of our lives that may need to be let go, at least for the moment.

This is like our lives. If our energy is not clear, then the world will probably not respond the way we want it to, because we are attached to the outcome. Your life is what it is now, so live in it as it is from the inside out to experience the clarity of thinking and focus you can bring to the moment.

The Reinvention Equation

Thomas Hanna says, "It is the inner change in brain function that makes possible outer change in muscle function." Hanna describes and teaches how to engage the brain in muscle movement. He provides specific exercises in his groundbreaking book *Somatics: Reawakening the Mind's Control of Movement, Flexibility, and Health.* When he wrote this book, the study of the brain and its functions was still in its infancy. Today much more is known about the flexibility of the brain and the power we have over making our neural patterns fire in a new way. Hanna is clear that events of a physical, mental, or emotional nature have a direct impact on the body and its healthy function. We know now, based on scientific research, that when events happen, whether they are traumatic or not, we have the power to monitor our reactions and choose our actions going forward.

When trauma happens, whether it be a job loss, health crisis, or the ending of a significant relationship, we are kicked out of life as we know it. The options of how to handle the situation may create stress, sadness, anger, and remorse. However, the choice of how to proceed is ours.

It is difficult to describe with words exactly the power we have. There is a magnificence in us that is available to us at all times. Over time we have forgotten (amnesia) this magnificence, instead leading our lives from ego and adapted habitual patterns. We humans have so much wisdom, intelligence, and connection to the universe beyond our physical selves. We hardly know how magnificent we are unless we take the time for this reinvention journey, which provides a glimpse of what is possible for us.

The reinvention equation is a powerful tool to regain the understanding of your essential nature and the breadth of options you have to live your life no matter the circumstances.

Once you understand the wholeness of who you are, then you must live your life in alignment to achieve the results you want. The Buddha said, "Commit not a single unwholesome action." I interpret this to mean living with awareness and in alignment with your essential self.

May your journey of reinvention be the best thing you have ever done for yourself. I hope we meet on the path of life to share our stories of reinvention.

The following quote from Jim Rohn is appropriate, I think, to close: "Don't wish it was easier, wish you were better. Don't wish for less problems, wish for more skills. Don't wish for less challenge, wish for more wisdom."

May you be well on your journey.

References

Childre, Doc, Howard Martin, Deborah Rozman, and Rollin McCraty. *Heart Intelligence*. Cardiff, Waterfront Press, 2016.

Doidge, Norman. *The Brain That Changes Itself.* New York, Penguin Books, 2007.

Goldstein, Elisha. *The Now Effect.* New York, Simon and Schuster, 2012.

Hanna, Thomas. *Somatics: Reawakening the Mind's Control of Movement, Flexibility, and Health.* Boston, Da Capo, 1988.

Hanson, Rick. *Buddha's Brain.* Oakland, New Harbinger Publications, 2009.

Leonard, George. *Mastery.* New York, Plume, 1992.

Leonard, George, and Michael Murphy. *The Life We Are Given.* New York, Penguin, 1995.

Mate, Gabour. *In the Realm of Hungry Ghosts.* Toronto, Vintage Canada, 2009.

Miller, Andrea. *Buddha's Daughter's: Teachings from Women Who Are Shaping Buddhism in the West.* Boulder, Shambhala Publications, 2014.

Neff, Kristin. *Self-Compassion*. New York, Harper Collins, 2011.

Ortner, Nick. *The Tapping Solution*. Carlsbad, Hay House, 2013.

Peterson, Martha. *Move without Pain*. New York, Sterling, 2011.

Siegel, Daniel J. *Mindsight: The New Science of Personal Transformation*. New York, Bantam Books, 2010.

Contact Howard

To get the latest updates
and resources, visit
www.howardjparsons.com

Twitter: twitter.com/HJPFacilitator

Facebook: facebook.com/
howard.parsons.54

Printed in the United States
By Bookmasters